# Faith, Science, and Society

# Books by Peter E. Hodgson

## Physics

*The Optical Model of Elastic Scattering.* Oxford: Clarendon Press, 1963.

*Nuclear Reactions and Nuclear Structure.* Oxford: Clarendon Press, 1971.

*Nuclear Heavy-Ion Reactions.* Oxford University Press, 1978.

*Growth Points in Nuclear Physics.* Vol. 1. Oxford: Pergamon Press, 1980.

*Growth Points in Nuclear Physics.* Vol. 2. Oxford: Pergamon Press, 1980.

*Growth Points in Nuclear Physics.* Vol. 3. Oxford: Pergamon Press, 1981.

*Nucleon Momentum and Density Distributions in Nuclei* (with A. N. Antonov and I. Zh. Petkov). Oxford: Clarendon Press, 1988.

*Spacetime and Electromagnetism* (with J. R. Lucas). Oxford: Clarendon Press, 1990.

*Pre-Equilibrium Nuclear Reactions* (with E. Gadioli). Oxford: Clarendon Press, 1991.

*Nucleon Correlations in Nuclei* (with A. N. Antonov and I. Zh. Petkov). Berlin: Springer-Verlag, 1993.

*The Nucleon Optical Potential.* Singapore: World Scientific, 1994.

*Introductory Nuclear Physics* (with E. Gadioli and E. Gadioli-Erba). Oxford University Press, 1996.

*Nuclear Physics* (with S. A. Sofianos). Pretoria: University of South Africa, 1997.

## Physics and Society

*Nuclear Physics in Peace and War.* London: Burns and Oates, 1961.

*Our Nuclear Future?* Belfast: Christian Journals, 1983.

*Science and Christianity.* Tokyo: Kinseido, 1992.

*Energy and Environment.* Tokyo: Kinseido, 1995.

*Energy and Environment.* London: Bowerdean, 1997.

*Science, Technology and Society.* Tokyo: Kinseido, 1999.

*Nuclear Power, Energy and the Environment.* London: Imperial College Press, 1999.

*Christianity and Science.* Johannesburg: St Augustine College, 2002.

*The Roots of Science and Its Fruits.* London: Saint Austin Press, 2003.

*Science and Belief in the Nuclear Age.* Naples, FL: Sapientia Press, 2005.

*Theology and Modern Physics.* Aldershot: Ashgate Publishing, 2005.

# Faith, Science, and Society

PETER E. HODGSON

*Sapientia* Press
of Ave Maria University

Sapientia Press
of Ave Maria University
5050 Ave Maria Blvd.
Ave Maria, FL 34142
888-343-8607

Cover Design: Eloise Anagnost

Cover Images *(clockwise from bottom)*:
Busy Commuters © EML, Shutterstock.com
Science Illustration © Sebastian Kaulitzki, Dreamstime.com
Prayer © Kuzma, Shutterstock.com

Printed in the United States of America.

Library of Congress Control Number: 2007940924

ISBN: 978-1-932589-46-7

# Table of Contents

## V. Philosophy of Science

# Preface

IN ANCIENT TIMES the activities of the natural philosophers had little connection with the everyday life of the people. They speculated about the entities that lie behind sensible appearances and about the reasons why things are what they are. Quite independently, craftsmen gained extensive knowledge of the properties of wood and stone, minerals and metals. This was purely empirical knowledge, based on experience and trial and error. Their great achievements owed nothing to the speculations of the natural philosophers.

The two types of activity started to come together in the 19th century, and by the 20th century they interacted strongly. The scientists, as the natural philosophers were by then called, showed how the efficiency of steam engines could be improved, and they developed a whole range of new materials—alloys and plastics, for example—that greatly enlarged the number of things that could be made. Into the 20th century, they discovered vast new realms of phenomena, such as radioactivity, nuclear reactions, and lasers, which soon found applications in medical treatment, in nuclear weapons and nuclear power, and in novel forms of lighting. The craftsmen made increasingly accurate and sophisticated apparatus for the scientists and thus made possible a whole new range of investigations. This in turn made possible new studies of the natural world. This cooperative interaction between scientists and craftsmen continued and grew throughout the 20th century and transformed our lives, so that our civilisation is unlike any other.

Naturally this gave rise to a whole range of problems, and some of these are discussed in the essays in this book. First of all there are the theological beliefs that made the whole development possible. It was the Judeo-Christian beliefs about the natural world, that it is good, orderly, contingent, and open to the human mind, that made possible the development of modern science, quite distinct from the primitive science of earlier times. This process began in the Middle Ages and came to maturity in the Renaissance. The Christian beliefs about the dignity of man also led to the first industrial revolution in medieval times. Several aspects of these theological questions are discussed in the first section. More details are given in the following historical section, together with brief accounts of some notable scientists.

One of the most dramatic examples of the effects of discoveries in pure science is provided by nuclear physics, which made possible not only devastating nuclear weapons but also the prospect of clean, reliable, safe, and relatively cheap nuclear power. This has led to many discussions about the effects on the environment and the effects of nuclear radiation. These discussions are not only technical but are strongly influenced by political considerations. Some of these contentious issues are discussed in the third section.

The discoveries and theories of modern physics, particularly those relating to quantum mechanics, have led to many speculations about God and the quantum world. This is connected with the various interpretations of quantum mechanics, as described in the fourth section.

These discussions, in turn, have led to renewed interest in the philosophy of science. What is science, how is it really done, and what is the status of its conclusions? How certain are scientific results, and do they have philosophical and even theological implications? These and other related questions are considered in the fifth section.

Governments are very sensitive to public opinion, and so they are subject to strong pressure to make decisions that they know are not in the best interests of society. It remains a necessary but uphill task for scientists and technologists to make their voices heard.

This study of modern science, its relation to faith, and its interactions with society shows that it is a richly human enterprise shot through with human values. It depends for its very existence on spiritual values, such as the existence of objective truth, the order of nature, the freedom of the individual, and the belief in cooperation. Without these beliefs it would never have started, could not continue, and would suffer speedy extinction. Scientific research is not carried out by robots but by living men and women who experience all the trials and tribulations of life, suffer the same fears and hopes, but in addition have something very special to offer society through their experience of scientific research.

The essays in this book were written on various occasions over several decades, and they may serve to highlight some of the problems we face today. There is some duplication, and this was allowed to remain so that each article stands on its own. Additional information on the subjects discussed may be found in two previous books, *The Roots of Science and Its Fruits* (London: Saint Austin Press, 2003) and *Science and Belief in the Nuclear Age* (Naples, Florida: Sapientia Press, 2005), and also in *Theology and Modern Physics* (Aldershot: Ashgate Publishing, 2005).

# Acknowledgments

I AM GRATEFUL to the editors and publishers of the following journals for their kind permission to reprint articles: *Blackfriars, Catholic Herald, Epworth Review, Faith, St Austin Review, Fellowship of Catholic Scholars Quarterly, Month, Newman,* and *Tablet.*

# PART I
# Theology

# CHAPTER 1

# Science without Christianity?

WE ARE ALL very familiar with the applications of modern science. They affect our lives in numerous ways and make our civilisation quite different from any of the other great civilisations that have flourished during the long history of the world. Daily life in ancient Egypt or China, for example, was in many ways quite different from our own. Why is this? Why did science as we know it fail to develop in all ancient civilisations?

To answer this question we need to understand how modern science came into being in the first place. This must depend on the way we think about the world. Science cannot begin without certain definite beliefs about matter, in particular that it is worthwhile to study it and that it is orderly and behaves in a reasonable way, so that anything we find out one day is still true the next. This order in the natural world must not be believed to be logically necessary, for then we would try to find out about it just by thinking, and we would never make experiments. Since it is difficult to find out about the world, we also need a strong motivation to keep us going when things become difficult.

If we study the beliefs of the ancient civilisations, we find that those beliefs were quite different in many ways, so we can see that our science could not begin in them. Science began in our civilisation because Catholic theology provided just those essential beliefs about the material world.

We believe that the world is good because it was made by God: 'God saw all that He had made, and indeed it was very good' (Genesis 1:31). This was further emphasised by the Incarnation, when Christ became man. His body was made of matter: 'The Word was made flesh and He lived among us' (John 1:14). God told us to study the world when He told us, 'Be fruitful, multiply, fill the earth and conquer it' (Genesis 1:28).

God need not have created the world, but He freely chose to do so, and He made it in the way He chose. If we want to find out about it, we have to study it directly, and that means making experiments.

The motivation to study the world is provided by the praise of wisdom in the Old Testament and by the parable of the talents in the New. As soon as it is realised that science helps us to grow more food and improve medical care, this motivation is reinforced because of our duty to feed the hungry and to give drink to the thirsty.

Catholic theology thus contains all the essential beliefs about the material world that are needed for the development of science. They may seem obvious to us; that is because we are living in a Christian civilisation. They would not have seemed obvious to people living in the ancient civilisations, and that is why science never developed in them.

Modern science flowered in the Renaissance, but this was preceded by its birth and early growth in medieval times. During the Middle Ages the writings of the ancient Greeks became available and stimulated intense theological and philosophical debate. Catholic thinkers used many of the ideas of the Greeks but did not accept them if they disagreed with Christian revelation. In particular, the Greek philosopher Aristotle had ideas about the world that effectively prevented the development of science, and these were swept away. Buridan, working in Paris, realised that Aristotle's ideas about motion were wrong, and the Christian doctrine of creation led him to develop his concept of impetus, which lies at the heart of dynamics and thus of all science. So we can see clearly how Catholic theology was crucial to the birth of modern science.

Subsequently, many misunderstandings arose, and some of them are still around today. But this does not affect the essential truth that science is Christian in its very essence. Before the coming of Christianity there was no science as we know it. Science was born in the Christian Middle Ages, and without the bedrock of Christian beliefs, it would wither away. Indeed, there can be no science without Christianity.

# CHAPTER 2

# Purpose in God, Man, and Nature

EVERY SINGLE human being has a unique genetic makeup, different from that of all the billions of people who have ever walked on the earth. Each of us is special, unique. As it is on the biological level, so it is on the spiritual. God has made us for a special purpose, different from that of all others. God calls us, and we respond. It is our purpose in life, our vocation, to follow God's call.

How do we know God's plan for us? Some people are singularly blessed: They know from an early age exactly what they want to do. They are driven by a sense of purpose. Some just know; others are inspired by events. A colleague of mine decided when he was quite young that he wanted to be the Regius Professor of Greek at the University of Oxford; it took him just about forty years to achieve his purpose. The schoolboy Michael Ventris heard a lecture by Sir Arthur Evans on the ancient Minoan civilisation in Crete and learned that no one knew how to read their writings. He resolved to solve the puzzle, and many years later he succeeded. Others have the ambition to be a great scientist, or a prime minister, or a famous writer, or to amass a great fortune.

Such ambitions, even if achieved, are rarely fully satisfying. 'The little toy, so fiercely sought, has lost its charms by being caught.' We are never content with what we have, and we want more and more. Eventually we may come to realise that we will never be satisfied, and we may realise that the reason is that 'our hearts are restless till they rest in Thee'.

Others are not so fortunate; they do not have even a limited purpose. They drift aimlessly from one thing to another, never get anywhere, and cannot see the way ahead. The rolling stone gathers no moss. They may not even try. That is the road to hell.

Others sincerely want to do the will of God but cannot see how they can best do it. Midst the encircling gloom, like Newman, they do not ask to see the distant scene; they can only put their hands into the hand of God, and ask only to be shown the next step. A journey of a thousand miles begins with a single step, and to know the direction of that first step is all we need to know. God knows His plan for us, and He decides how much we need to know.

Sometimes we think we know which way to go, and our plans collapse. We fail a vital examination or do not win a coveted scholarship. Failure is not always a disaster; often it is God's way of telling us which way He wants us to go. It is as much a tragedy to pass an examination that we should have failed as it is to fail an examination we should have passed. The brilliant boy who passes effortlessly through school, winning all the prizes, can come to believe that success is his due. When he arrives at university, he encounters a different scene, and he may find the going more difficult. He has to learn how to cope with failure. It may be just a signpost to the future.

Sometimes we are faced with a stark choice. We are devoting our life to a very worthy and agreeable purpose that earns the respect and admiration of those to whom we are responsible. Then suddenly God intervenes and shows us that what we are doing is too cosy and self-centred. Instead, He points to a higher stony path that is our only way to salvation. Mother Teresa was a respected teacher in a prestigious high school in India but realised that it was not enough. She decided to devote the rest of her life to serving the poorest of the poor. She was told that she was doing such excellent work teaching schoolgirls from rich families who were destined for influential careers that it would be foolish to give it all up. She disregarded this advice and gave her life to the poor. Franz Jagerstatter was an Austrian leading a quiet life devoted to his wife and family. Then he was summoned to join the Nazi army, which he saw was evil. He decided to refuse. He was told by his parish priest that he and his family would suffer if he disobeyed the commands of the authorities. He refused to go against his conscience and was executed. Oscar Romero, initially a rather shy and conservative bishop, had his eyes opened by the murder of Fr Rutilio Grande, together with an old man and a young boy, as they were on their way to celebrate Mass. He realised that he was called to defy the authorities and stand by the poor, to be the defender of the oppressed and the voice of those who had no voice. He knew that he was hated by the rich and powerful and that his life was in danger. He was frightened but carried on, saying that 'if they kill me, I will rise again in the Salvadoran people'. After three years he was shot.

It may happen that God makes it quite clear what He wants us to do, and we don't like it at all. We have other ideas, and, like Jonah, we run off in another direction and have to be brought back by drastic means. We may flee the Hound of Heaven down the arches of the years, but those strong feet follow us 'with unhurrying chase and unperturbed pace, deliberate speed, majestic instancy' and, with a Voice above the beat: 'Lo, all things betray thee, who betrayest Me!' brings us back to His chosen way.

This insistent call can guide us in many less obvious ways. We know what God wants us to do, but we are tired and decide we need a break. We have all the means to enjoy ourselves; there seems nothing wrong with our lives. We ought to be happy, but we still feel a general unease and certainly are not happy. Then eventually we pull ourselves together and force ourselves to start God's work again. As we go on, our interest revives, and after a few hours, we begin to feel better. At the end of the day, we feel a sense of achievement and are tired but happy again.

If we attain our purpose we may be satisfied for a time, particularly if our purpose is a high and noble one. We may become proud of our own achievements. This is a time to realise that we can do nothing on our own without the power of God: 'I am the vine and you are the branches; without Me you can do nothing' (John 15:5). We may plan our lives carefully, have definite plans, and pray for the means to carry them out. Prayer is always answered, and the answer is usually no. Years later, we reflect that it would have been a disaster if our prayer had been answered in the way we wanted. Our lives are in hands stronger than our own.

It is always salutary to ask ourselves what is the purpose behind our actions; often it is not what we think it is, or what we would like others to think it is. The Pharisees who dropped money ostentatiously into the corban were thinking more of the reputation they would gain than the needs of the Temple. Do we always give our money or help as secretly as possible? If we offer to help a neighbour, are we motivated by curiosity about his lifestyle? Do we accept membership of a committee more to gain political power than to serve the community? Our actions are so often tainted by a hidden—or not-so-hidden—purpose in addition to the ostensive one.

At other times God's purpose is hidden from us, and indeed if we did but know it, we would set about achieving that purpose only by steadfastly following a quite different way. Thus scientists try to find out about the world but are quite unable to foresee the results, not only within science itself, but especially concerning their effects on human society. Their vocation is to seek the truth about the natural world: No other motive is acceptable. It may sound strange to say it, but in the course of their work scientists must never have the aim of benefiting mankind. One famous scientist has declared that if any of his students ever said that he was doing his research in order to benefit mankind, that student would immediately be thrown out of his laboratory. Any work undertaken with that purpose is certain to be mediocre; indeed, it is nothing less than the prostitution of science. History confirms this, as research devoted to fundamental understanding often has great and entirely unexpected benefits. Conrad Roentgen wanted to find out about electrical discharges in gases: He discovered X-rays. He would never have done this if his purpose had been to improve methods of medical diagnosis. Marie Curie studied radioactivity and discovered radium. She would never have done this if she had sought a cure for cancer. Ernest Rutherford studied nuclear reactions and thought that they would never have more than small-scale applications.

It is only after the scientific discovery has been made and we see that it can be applied to benefit mankind that another responsibility and purpose become evident. Then we must use our new knowledge to feed the hungry, to give drink to the thirsty, and to clothe the naked.

In this way science has an immense impact on our lives, but this is made possible only by scientists motivated solely by the desire to understand, and then by technologists who purposefully devote their lives to using the discoveries of the scientists to improve our lives.

It is the same with literary composition. Dorothy Sayers, when writing her plays on the life of Christ, emphasised that her purpose was not to be edifying but simply to tell a story. 'A work of art that is not good and true in art is not good or true in any other respect, and is useless for any purpose whatsoever—even for edification—because it is a lie, and the devil is the father of all such'.

To be effective, purpose must be steely and sustained. Nothing worthwhile is achieved easily, and almost fanatical determination is needed to overcome all the obstacles in our way. Marie Curie slaved away for years purifying tons of pitchblende to obtain a speck of radium, ruining her health in the process. Johannes Kepler decided to determine the orbit of the planet Mars, and this required over twenty years of laborious calculation, with none of the modern devices to lighten the burden. He accepted the Aristotelian view that the orbit must be a circle, but however hard he tried he could not get a circle to fit within the accuracy of the measurements. He could fit a circle to within about ten minutes of arc, but this was not good enough because the measurements were accurate to within two or three minutes of arc. Eventually he faced the staggering truth that it was not a circle but an ellipse and so opened the way to Newtonian dynamics. This was achieved only by a steely purpose sustained for years on end.

It is all too easy to underestimate the amount of hard work that is necessary to enable one to make a serious contribution to science. This is particularly so when several different disciplines are involved. Thus many people have views on the relation between science on the one hand and theology and philosophy on the other. Duhem once attended a conference devoted to such problems and was horrified by the nonsense he heard. Eventually he declared that 'if we want to handle with competence and fruitfully the questions in the domain common to metaphysics and positive science, let us begin by studying the latter for ten, for fifteen years; let us study it, first of all, in itself and for itself, without seeking to put it into harmony with such and such philosophical assertion; then, as we have mastered its principles, applied it in a thousand ways, we can search for its metaphysical meaning, which will not fail to accord with true philosophy.' Therefore, if they 'had not become men with deep scientific knowledge they must remain silent'.

If, in spite of all, we still seem to be achieving nothing, we can but put our trust in God. He knows what He is about. We can serve His purpose in ways that are hidden to us if only we strive always to do His will. In sickness or in health, in success or in failure, we can serve His purpose. We may not understand now, but eventually the pattern will be revealed to us.

The scientific study of the universe reveals God's purpose. The more we know about the world, the more it seems that we are unique in the universe. Ours is a privileged planet with properties so special, so exceedingly improbable, that it is unlikely that there is another like it. There are questions yet to be answered in the future, but meanwhile we can rejoice that God made such a wondrously beautiful world.

If, in spite of all our efforts, we still seem to be achieving nothing, we can but put our trust in God. We can recall the words of Newman:

> God has created me to do Him some definite service; He has committed some work to me which He has not committed to another. I have my mission—I may never know it in this life, but I shall be told it in the next. Somehow I am necessary for His purposes. I have a part in His great work; I am a link in a chain, a bond of connection between persons. He has not created me for naught. I shall do good, I shall do His work; I shall be an angel of peace; a preacher of truth in my own place, while not intending it, if I do but keep His commandments and serve Him in my calling.
>
> Therefore I will trust Him. Whatever, wherever I am, I can never be thrown away. If I am in sickness, my sickness may serve

Him; if I am in sorrow, my sorrow may serve Him. My sickness, or perplexity, or sorrow may be the necessary causes of some great end, which is quite beyond us. He does nothing in vain; he may prolong my life, He may shorten it; He knows what He is about. He may take away my friends; he may throw me among strangers. He may make me feel desolate, make my spirits sink, hide the future from me—still He knows what He is about.

We can serve His purpose in ways that are hidden to us if only we strive always to do His will. In sickness or in health, in success or in failure, we can serve His purpose. We may not understand now, but eventually the pattern will be revealed to us.

It may happen that although we know our purpose in life, and follow it faithfully, everything we do seems to end in failure. We may then recall a far-off figure whose life, by all earthly standards, was an abject failure. He was a vagrant, despised and rejected by men. He occupied no high office in Church or state, was awarded no prizes or diplomas, wrote no books or articles, and often had no place to lay His head. He was accused and condemned and finally was executed in the most brutal way. But after His death came the Easter dawn, and He has had more effect on history than any other man.

# CHAPTER 3

# The Purpose of It All[*]

WHAT IS the purpose of it all? Is it all, in Whitehead's memorable phrase, just 'the hurrying of material, endlessly, meaninglessly'? Or is there a purpose of the universe, and for each one of us? From Socrates defending purpose against the atomists to modern scientists enunciating the anthropic principle, this is still the vital question. A sense of purpose invests our lives with meaning; without it, there is only aimless futility. Whatever we do, whatever we achieve is vulnerable to the devastating question: 'So what?' and we cannot rest without an answer.

Professor Stanley L. Jaki, a Benedictine priest with doctorates in systematic theology and nuclear physics, is well equipped to answer these questions. He reminds us that the only fully satisfactory answer is found in the realisation that, in Newman's words, 'God has created me to do Him some definite service; He has committed some work to me which He has not committed to another. I have my mission—I may never know it in this life, but I shall be told it in the next.' We may try to avoid God's purpose, we may follow other paths and other goals, but in the end we realise that 'all things betray thee, who betrayest Me'.

But how do we know that this is true? Secularists propose other answers, apparently much more definite and practical. Does not science hold out a vision of uninterrupted progress for the human race,

---

[*] Peter Hodgson, review of *The Purpose of It All*, by Stanley L. Jaki, *Tablet* (24 August 1991): 1028.

and is not the furthering of this endeavour a purpose worthy enough to claim all our efforts? This might plausibly have been held in the last century, but not now, when it is evident that science and technology cannot alone ensure happiness.

To support the Christian answer, Paley pointed to the order in nature as evidence of the Great Designer. The logic of the argument was weakened by Darwin, who attributed the diversity of living forms to the selection among chance variations by impersonal forces. Darwin carefully concealed his rank materialism, and the popularity of his books indicated that they satisfied a deep-seated need in Victorian society. The hidden agenda surfaced when Aldous Huxley welcomed the political and moral liberation experienced in a meaningless world.

Considered as a scientific theory, Jaki points out, evolution still lacks proof in all but the simplest cases. We are still far from understanding the complexities of a single cell, let alone a whole organism. Whatever understanding may be achieved in the future, it will still provide evidence of design.

Cosmological studies have shown the astonishing specificity of the universe. If the conditions at the time of the Big Bang had been even slightly different, life would have been impossible, so it seems as if the universe was made just for human habitation. Faced with this remarkable fact, three responses are possible: the recognition of a Creator, dismissal of the findings as 'thought-provoking', and recourse to the claim that the observer makes the universe what it is. Behind the latter response is the idea that there are many universes, with life arising only in those with the required characteristics, which few consider plausible.

The idea that sentient life arises whenever the conditions are right has led to fruitless searches for extraterrestrial intelligences. But if this is true, then why did science itself not arise in ancient civilisations with all the material requirements? The only convincing explanation is to be found in nonmaterial factors, principally the Christian belief in the creation of the universe out of nothing. It was from this starting point that Buridan and Oresme were led to the fundamental concepts of dynamics that lie at the basis of all science.

Since scientific research is a not purposeful activity, Jaki considers it more than curious that scientists like Monod and Dawkins should maintain that all processes in nature are based on chance, a notion that is never analysed. Analogies with computer programs fail to emphasise that the results are strictly determined by the program itself and the initial conditions, both requiring explanation. Basic to the argument advanced by Dawkins is the claim that elementary particles are so simple that they require no explanation, a remark that would surprise particle physicists familiar with their extreme specificity.

The most fundamental question is the freedom of the will. If our thoughts are determined solely by the motions of the atoms in our brains, then no meaning can be assigned to them. The apparent licensing of free will by Heisenberg's uncertainty principle was soon recognised as nonsense by Eddington, among others.

Jaki argues that all attempts either to establish or to discredit purpose on the basis of scientific results are bound to fail. The purpose of life and the foundation of science are to be found only in the biblical recognition that we are created by God with a purpose and with the freedom to accept or reject that purpose. Even secularists like Bertrand Russell and H. G. Wells, after lifetimes spent undermining Christian belief, acknowledged in the end that it is the main hope for mankind.

This brief summary can only indicate a few of the topics that are discussed by Professor Jaki with his customary skill and immense learning. He is acutely sensitive to the treacherous philosophies lurking beneath popular writings about science and is able to evaluate them at their true worth in the light of Christian principles. Like most of his work, his book is hardly an easy read, but it will be found richly rewarding by all who are concerned to find the purpose of it all.

### Reference

Stanley L. Jaki, *The Purpose of It All* (Washington, DC: Regnery Publishing, Inc., 1991).

# CHAPTER 4

## Leaps of Faith

IT IS WELL-KNOWN that people who are attracted to the Catholic faith often hesitate before taking the final step and ask to be received into what Newman called the 'One True Fold of the Redeemer'. In the 19th century many in this situation wrote to Newman for his advice, and some of the resulting correspondence has now been published in the book *Newman to Converts* by Fr Stanley L. Jaki.[1] Newman was sensitively aware of their difficulties, and while they were unsure he strongly advised them to wait. Many thought that they should read more books and consider more arguments, but Newman warned them that this road has no end, and life is too short for it. The moment of grace comes once, and as soon as one is sure, there should be no hesitation. It requires a leap of faith, supported by the grace of God.

Once the leap is made, the difficulties disappear. It is like looking at a stained-glass window from the inside instead of from the outside. Or it is like wandering in a maze—when you reach the centre you know that you are there without a shadow of doubt. In all his long life as a Catholic, and in spite of many trials and tribulations, Newman never had the slightest doubt that he had made the right decision, saying that the hand of God was wonderfully over him.

---

[1] Stanley L. Jaki, *Newman to Converts* (Port Huron, MI: Real-View Books, 2001).

A somewhat similar experience happens as science advances. There may be an excellent theory that accounts very well for a large number of experiments, and yet as time goes by, exceptions are found. As these exceptions increase in number, and it is more and more difficult to explain them away, it becomes clear that the theory is not good enough to account for the experienced reality. In such circumstances it is not possible to proceed logically and deduce a better theory on the basis of the old. A fresh start is needed, and this requires a leap of imagination by the scientist. Once he has made this leap, and achieved a new insight into reality, he can then deduce its consequences and test them against the facts that were explained by the old theory and also those that were not. If it all fits, the new theory can take the place of the old. The old theory still remains valid over a limited range but nevertheless is recognised as radically unsound and no longer acceptable when considering the whole of our experiences. A prime example of this is the transition from Newtonian to Einsteinian dynamics.

Such an analogy has several similarities to the process of religious conversion. While Newman was quite clear that he had entered the one true fold, he nevertheless continued to recognise that there is much holiness in the Anglican Church, just as the physicist still recognises the validity of Newtonian dynamics for phenomena involving velocities small compared with that of light. Also important is that in neither case is there a clear logical path from the old to the new. Thus in religious conversion, God does not force us: He gives us sufficient grace to make our own free choice. This grace is available to all who seek the truth. Scientists are not so strongly favoured; very few have the ability to make major advances, though many more scientists can make smaller advances that gradually increase our knowledge of reality.

# CHAPTER 5

# Now I See!

WE ALL HAVE the experience of trying to recall a forgotten name. We rarely succeed while we are thinking hard about it, but often hours later the name suddenly comes to mind, and we recognise instantly that it is correct. Somehow the name must have been in our mind all along, but we could not find it.

We have a similar experience when we try to solve a problem. We examine it by all the methods we can think of, but to no avail. We finally give up; but when we wake up the next morning, we immediately see the solution.

Teachers have similar experiences. We carefully explain an idea to a pupil, only to be met with a blank look. All we can do is to repeat it, and eventually the pupil will suddenly say, 'Aha, now I see!' The whole process is profoundly mysterious. Even the best teachers will admit that they do not know how they do it.

There are many examples of this in the accounts that scientists give of how they made their discoveries. The chemist Kekulé was trying to find the structure of benzene. He knew the atoms that made up the benzene molecule, but however he arranged them, his configurations did not fit the known facts. That night when he was asleep he had a dream where he saw snakes writhing around. Then one of the snakes caught hold of its own tail, to make a ring. Immediately Kekulé saw that the structure of benzene was a ring of carbon atoms.

The same thing happens with mathematics. The French mathematician Henri Poincaré was studying what became known as Fuchsian functions, but the key concept eluded him. Then suddenly, when he was getting on a bus, the solution came to him. It was then just a matter of working out the solution in detail. In a rather similar way the Irish mathematician William Hamilton was trying to find out how to multiply quaternions. He told his family what he was doing, and every morning they asked him whether he had succeeded. Each time he had to say no. Then one day he was out walking, and suddenly the solution came to him; he was so excited that he scratched it onto the bridge he was crossing.

The great scientist Newton was once asked how he made his discoveries. 'By setting my mind continually unto the problem', he replied. The conditions for success seem to be first a period of hard study when all aspects of the problem are carefully reviewed, followed by a period of relaxation. During that period the unconscious mind continually works on the problem, though we are not aware of it, and when it finds the solution, it breaks through into our conscious mind and gives us the answer.

The historian of science Stillman Drake has spent many years studying Galileo. He has translated several of Galileo's books and correspondence and is very familiar with his life. He knew that Galileo was well thought of by several cardinals and two grand dukes of Tuscany and that he held professorships in two universities. Galileo was also a very careful man, not given to making statements without careful study. All this did not fit in with the commonly accepted opinion that Galileo was an impetuous, irresponsible firebrand opposed to the Church. Drake then suddenly realised that Galileo's professions of devotion to the Church were not just conventional platitudes but sincere expressions of belief and that he was a devout Catholic who tried to prevent the Church from making a serious error. His opponents were not the theologians but the Aristotelian philosophers, and he saw that there was a real danger that they would convince the Church authorities to condemn the heliocentric theory of Copernicus, which would cause grave scandal when that theory was eventually proved to be true, as indeed happened. This is an example of how we can suddenly see a problem in a different way that we realise is the right way. Another example is provided by the way Galileo suddenly saw that the heliocentric theory gave a better account of all the available data than the geocentric theory.

Further examples are provided by conversion. St Paul had persecuted the Church for years and suddenly saw that he was fighting against the truth. Newman had a similar experience. Ten days after his reception into what he called the one true fold of Christ, he told a friend that the conviction of the catholicity of the Church of Rome had broken 'suddenly and clearly' on his mind six years earlier. The grace of conversion is a gift of God, but the mental processes are similar in all the cases mentioned.

# CHAPTER 6

# Science and the Loss of Faith

IT IS NO SURPRISE that young people are immensely impressed by science and the technological marvels that it makes possible. Scientists study the natural world carefully and objectively, and what they find out is certainly true. By contrast, other subjects learnt at school seem to be largely a matter of opinion and hearsay, to be believed on trust. The Bible comes into this category, and the contrast with science soon convinces them that the Bible is just a collection of fables.

In his autobiography, Einstein recalls that he had a religious upbringing, but his religious beliefs came to an abrupt end when he was twelve. He recalls that 'through the reading of popular scientific books I soon reached the conviction that much of the stories of the Bible could not be true. . . . Suspicion against every kind of authority grew out of this experience'.

More recently, Francis Crick has said, 'I realised early on that it is detailed scientific knowledge which makes certain religious beliefs untenable. A knowledge of the true age of the earth and of the fossil record makes it impossible for any balanced intellect to believe in the truth of every part of the Bible in the way that fundamentalists do. And if some of the Bible is manifestly wrong, why should any of the rest of it be accepted automatically? A belief, at the time it was formulated, may not only have appealed to the imagination but also fit well with all that was then known. It can nevertheless be made to appear ridiculous because of facts uncovered later by science. What could be more foolish than to base one's entire view of life on ideas that, however plausible at the time, now appear to be quite erroneous?'

In saying this, he accurately reflects what many people think today, and indeed parts of it are quite correct. Modern science does make the beliefs of the fundamentalist untenable. We have to be careful when we maintain that the Bible is true and emphasise that by this we say that it is true in the sense intended by God. Like any text, its genre must be understood. It is not a scientific report and does not make scientific statements. Its purpose is to teach us truths necessary for the conduct of our lives and for our salvation.

This is well-known in other contexts. If we read in a poem about a tiger, tiger burning bright, we would be very dim if we thought that it meant that the tiger was on fire. Similarly when we read about the right hand of God, we do not think that we are being told that God has hands.

It is very important that these simple truths about how to interpret different types of literature are explained as clearly as possible to young children, for otherwise they are very likely to go the way of Einstein and Crick. There is nothing new about this; the principles of biblical interpretation were formulated centuries ago by St Augustine and St Thomas Aquinas. The Church has the continuing authority to interpret the Bible, and she would never do so in a way that contradicts established science. Indeed, science can assist in the task of biblical interpretation.

It is regrettably true that some theologians have made serious mistakes and have declared that the Bible makes some statements about the natural world that we now know are untrue. The Galileo case is a notorious example of this and serves as a warning to take care when interpreting the Bible. In his defence against the charge that he was supporting a scientific theory that was in conflict with the Bible, Galileo reiterated the principles of Augustine and Aquinas, and Pope John Paul II has declared that in this matter Galileo was sounder than the theologians appointed to judge him. He admitted that Galileo was treated unjustly, and he praised his views on the relation between science and religion.

# CHAPTER 7

# God the Mathematician

OVER THE LAST few centuries, scientists have found that the physical world can be described very accurately by mathematics. The motions of projectiles on the earth and of the planets round the sun are described by Newton's laws, electrical and magnetic phenomena by Maxwell's equations, and the atomic and nuclear realms by Schrödinger's equation. These equations are very simple mathematically and can easily be solved to give the behaviour of simple systems. More-complicated systems can sometimes be solved by using high-speed computers, and it is found that the simple equations describe layer upon layer of extremely complicated phenomena.

This is really very surprising. Why should the physical world be describable by mathematics, and by such simple mathematics? The scientist Wigner expressed astonishment at the 'unreasonable effectiveness of mathematics'. What is the connection between mathematics, which exists in the mind, and the real objects of the natural world?

A similar problem is the relatively small number of fundamental building blocks that constitute our world. There are about 100 chemical elements, and the atoms of each element are made of different numbers of just three types of particle: protons, electrons, and neutrons. At a deeper level, there are quarks, gluons, and many evanescent particles.

Why are all hydrogen atoms exactly the same, and why are they all described by the same mathematics? What is the connection between them? If they are made in the same mould, then who made the mould? Since mathematics exists in the mind, the connection must be in a mind. Whose mind? Certainly not ours; we did not make the atoms. Inevitably we are led to see that the answer must be an altogether different type of mind, the mind of a being powerful enough to create matter and give it its properties. James Jeans famously declared that God is a mathematician, but that is an understatement. God creates matter and sustains it in being. In doing so, He gives matter definite properties, and these are described by mathematics. When he first became aware of the power of mathematics, Einstein remarked that it seemed to him 'a revelation of the Highest Author, and I will never forget it.'

The mind of God and His creative power pervade the universe, and this constitutes what may be called the theosphere, at a higher level than Teilhard de Chardin's noosphere. God has complete mastery over the matter He has created. Normally it continues to behave exactly according to its nature in a strictly deterministic way, but, if He wishes, God can impose His will directly on matter and cause it to do whatever He decides. This leaves open the possibility of miracles, and indeed there have been many instances of miracles, such as the healing of the sick at Lourdes and other places of pilgrimage, or in a more spectacular way, visible to thousands of people, the miracle of the sun at Fatima.

Why is matter described by such simple mathematics? God could easily have made a world that obeyed much more complicated equations, or a world governed by complicated forces, so that we would never be able to find out how it all works. As it is, it is just simple enough to allow us to succeed in understanding it but yet not so simple that it would not be a real challenge to try to do so. Obviously God created the world in such a way that we can find out about it. Not only is matter good, but it is open to the human mind. If we work hard enough, we can find at least some of its secrets. Research is an exciting, endless quest. God wanted there to be scientists willing to spend their lives studying His works.

CHAPTER 8

# Extraterrestrials

THE RECENT DISCOVERY of another star with at least one
planet has excited renewed discussion about the existence of
extraterrestrials. Much ink has already been spent on speculations about the possible existence of intelligent beings and
whole civilisations on other planets in the galaxy. There is an ongoing
project, called SETI (Search for Extra-Terrestrial Intelligence),
devoted to attempts to detect signals from people in such civilisations.
No other planet in our solar system is even remotely suitable for life as
we know it, and the other galaxies are much too far away ever to be
reached, so attention is concentrated on stars in our own galaxy. There
is increasing evidence that some of them have planets, so is it likely
that they have intelligent beings on them?

This possibility raises several theological questions. Do such
beings have immortal souls, and if so, how can they be saved? Does
Christ become incarnate in each of these civilisations when they reach
the appropriate stage of development?

Several attempts have been made, notably by using the Drake equation, to estimate the possibility of the existence of planets with intelligent beings that could communicate with us. One begins with the
number of stars in the galaxy, about 100 billion, and then reduces it by
a series of factors: the probability of a star having planets; the probability that one of these planets is able to support life; the probability that
life will actually develop; the probability that this life will evolve into

29

intelligent beings; and finally a factor to account for the limited lifetime of such a civilisation. Making guesstimates of all these factors, Drake found that there should be about 10,000 planets with civilisations capable of sending messages to us. Behind this argument is the Darwinian belief that whenever the physical conditions are suitable, the evolution of life and of mankind will take place.

It has recently been pointed out,[1] however, that several important factors have been left out of this argument, the most critical being the presence of the moon. It is generally accepted that life first began in tidal basins, and these depend on the moon. The formation of the moon is generally attributed to a glancing collision between an asteroid and the earth. For the moon to be formed from such a collision, several very unlikely conditions have to be satisfied. This reduces Drake's estimate by a factor of between a million and ten thousand million, making it a very unlikely event indeed.

There are many other factors concerning human history that also need to be taken into account, including the lives of physicists whose work made radio possible. The net result is that ETI is so improbable that it is not worth taking seriously. One of the most prominent Darwinists, Ernst Mayr, considers SETI to be a deplorable waste of money.

It is just as well that we are unlikely to be invaded by extraterrestrials, as they are likely to have far-superior technology and would simply eliminate us or make us their slaves. Theologians can find more sensible subjects for their speculations.

---

[1] Stanley L. Jaki, 'The Origin of the Earth-Moon System and the Rise of Scientific Intelligence' in *Numbers Decide, and Other Essays* (Port Huron, MI: Real-View Books, 2003), 143.

# PART II
# History

# CHAPTER 9

# Christianity and Technology in the Middle Ages

THE BEGINNINGS of technology, the making of things for practical use, occurred when the first man fashioned a crude axe by binding a sharp stone to the end of a stick. Later, he found out how to split flints to use as knives to cut meat or to make a better axe. He learned how to mould and fire clay to make pottery vessels.

If stone circles such as that of Stonehenge were indeed temples of worship, they provide early examples of the connection between religion and technology. The construction of such circles required the cooperation of hundreds of men to cut the stones from quarries and to transport them great distances by pulling them on rollers made from the trunks of trees.

Great advances in technology were made in the ancient civilisations, and some of their achievements are astonishing reminders of their skill. The pyramids of Egypt provide further examples of the connection between religion and technology, for they were built as tombs for the pharaohs and contained many objects for their use in the afterlife. The pyramids were most accurately aligned and skilfully planned. To cut and transport thousands of huge stone blocks, each weighing up to twenty tons, required the labour of armies of men for decades. The civilisations of Babylon and Assyria, Greece and Rome, also provide numerous examples of great architectural achievement.

These great civilisations began in Mesopotamia, and others occurred independently at around the same time in five regions of the earth, in the Indus Valley in India, in the Yellow River Valley in China, in Central America, and in the coastal plain of Peru. In other regions, where men lived for tens of thousands of years, such as sub-Saharan Africa, Australia, Polynesia, and North America, no comparable developments took place, and life remained unchanged for millennia. This difference has been attributed to differences in the climate, the availability of minerals, the flora and the possibility of growing crops, and the fauna, especially of animals that can be domesticated. These factors either facilitated or retarded the possibility of the development of a civilisation.

Another question is how the civilisations in these six regions developed further. If, knowing their histories up to a millennia or two ago, we had been asked which areas would experience further growth, we might choose China, which had a vastly superior technology. In Europe we might choose the Islamic civilisation, heir to Greece and Rome. None of these very reasonable predictions would be correct. What actually happened was that all these civilisations sooner or later became static or went into decline, while the most astonishing development in the whole of history took place in western Europe. Why was this?

In ancient civilisations, there was no shortage of manpower and no incentive to devise less labour-intensive methods. The energy needed for great buildings was provided by human and animal muscle. A remarkable change took place in the Middle Ages, when new ways were found to replace muscle power with machines. It was one of the most technologically innovative periods in human history. In every aspect of work great advances were made, so that it has been justly called the first industrial revolution. Several of these innovations had indeed been made in earlier civilisations, but they were first developed and welded together in the Middle Ages.

Christianity changed the whole attitude of man toward nature. The animistic belief that nature is governed by unpredictable spirits was replaced by the Christian doctrine of creation by God, who gave matter fixed properties, governed by laws that we can discover and use. This belief encouraged the development of science, and with it the growth of technology. These beliefs led to important innovations over the whole range of man's activities.

In the ancient world, farmers used oxen to draw the plough, and these were slow and inefficient. The scratch plough was replaced by the heavy plough, which turns the earth over and needs six or more oxen to draw it. In the Middle Ages, horses gradually replaced oxen, and the horse collar quadrupled their pulling power. Such a simple invention as the stirrup made it so much easier to ride and control a horse. It was more expensive to support horses, and this forced farmers to combine their efforts, which altered the structure of society. The whippletree ensured that the pulling force of a pair of horses was applied at the centre of a wagon, thus making it much easier to control, reducing the likelihood that the traces would be broken when turning. These advances vastly increased the productivity of the land, and with it the number of people it could support.

Monasteries were centres of technological innovation. In ancient times manual work was considered fit only for slaves and beneath the dignity of educated people. Christian theology changed this by extolling the virtue of work. At the same time it was believed that unnecessary work was to be avoided if possible by using our brains to see how the work could be done more efficiently, so as to leave time for prayer and more creative pursuits. This encouraged the invention of machines to replace the muscle power of man or beast.

Life in a monastery required prayer at set times throughout the day and night. The older methods of marking the passage of time, by sand and water clocks, proved insufficiently accurate, so much effort was devoted to making more accurate clocks. One of the earlier examples, with a sophisticated double-feedback mechanism, may be seen in the nave of Salisbury cathedral. It was only later that clocks were installed in the main squares of towns to regulate commerce and the hours of work.

Water power was also used to replace muscle power. Many monasteries were built near rivers or streams, and waterwheels ground the corn. The cam was used to transform rotary motion into linear motion and to operate saws and fulling machines. On flatter land, water power was replaced by windmills for the same purposes. Brass was first made at Tintern Abbey on the river Wye.

These and many other technological devices created and sustained feudal society and also transformed the nature of warfare. The stirrup put the whole weight of horse and rider behind the thrusting lance and so made the mounted horseman into a far-more-formidable fighting combination. Horsemen soon became the backbone of the army, and more and more were needed. Men were required to supply horses and riders for the army; to meet the high cost, Church property was confiscated and society was organised on feudal lines. The effectiveness of the army was further increased by the creative ingenuity of craftsmen who invented the arbalest and the trebuchet and eventually the musket and the cannon.

It is now recognised that modern science began in the Middle Ages, when for the first time in history there was a Christian society with beliefs about the natural world that provided the necessary presuppositions of science. At the same time, the extraordinary advances of technology were inspired by Christian beliefs about nature and the dignity of man. At that time science and technology were quite independent of each other, and this persisted through the second industrial revolution in the 19th century. It is only now, when we are in the midst of the third industrial revolution, that science and technology have come together, and their interaction has produced the world of today. Scientific research, motivated simply by the desire to understand the natural world in greater and greater detail, without any thought of practical application, has revealed the atomic and nuclear worlds and that of the elementary particles. The knowledge of electromagnetism and the properties of electrons have made possible radio, television, and the computers that have irreversibly changed our lives. A vital contribution to this has been made by Christian beliefs.

A century ago it was generally believed that nothing of significance for science took place in the Middle Ages, so that era could be ignored in any discussion of the history of science. This belief has now been completely demolished by the extensive researches of Pierre Duhem, Marshall Clagett, Edward Grant, Annalise Maier, Alistair Crombie, Lynn White, and many others who have provided extensive documentation of the pioneer work carried out at that time. Their work was not always welcome. The pioneer of medieval science studies was Pierre Duhem, and he wrote a vast treatise, *Le système du monde*, in 10 large volumes.

It is remarkable that, in spite of the massive scholarly work that has been done on medieval science, there are still books on the history of science that begin with an account of the achievements of the ancient Greeks and pass immediately to the Renaissance, completely ignoring the contribution of the Middle Ages. Such books may be immediately identified by the 'JCD test': Look in the index for the names Jaki, Crombie, and Duhem, three Catholic scholars who have devoted their lives to historical studies of science and have written many magisterial books, some of which are listed below. Scholars who are interested in the origin and development of science and its associated technology find in them a mine of vitally important information. If one disagrees with their findings, the scholarly response is to give reasons and initiate a dialogue. If, however, one is unwilling to accept what they say for some other reason, the response, as the example of Sarton showed, is the silent treatment. This is still strong today for other reasons. Is it not high time for honest scholars to give due weight to the achievements of the Middle Ages?

## References

Alistair Crombie. *Augustine to Galileo: The History of Science, A.D. 400–1650.* London: Falcon Press, 1952.

———. *Robert Grosseteste and the Foundations of Experimental Science, 1100–1700.* Oxford: Oxford University Press, 1953.

———. *Styles of Scientific Thinking in the European Tradition* (three volumes). London: Duckworth, 1994.

Pierre Duhem. *Etudes sur Leonardo da Vinci* (three volumes). Paris: A. Hermann, 1906–13.

———. *Le système du monde* (ten volumes). Paris: Hermann et Fils, 1913–59.

Stanley L. Jaki. *The Relevance of Physics*. Chicago: Chicago University Press, 1966.

———. *Science and Creation*. Edinburgh: Scottish Academic Press, 1974.

———. *The Road of Science and the Ways of God*. Edinburgh: Scottish Academic Press, 1978.

———. *Uneasy Genius: The Life and Work of Pierre Duhem*. Dordrecht: Martinus Nijhoff, 1984.

# CHAPTER 10

# Pierre Duhem: Historian of the Christian Origin of Modern Science[*]

IT IS STILL possible to find histories of science that describe the achievements of the ancient Greeks and then pass immediately to the Renaissance, with perhaps a brief remark about the absence of any development worth mentioning in the intervening period. That such slighting of the contributions of the medieval philosophers is no longer acceptable in any work with pretensions to scholarship is mainly due to the French physicist Pierre Duhem.

Duhem was born in Paris in 1861 and studied in the College Stanislaus and the Ecole Normale. While still in his second year, he submitted a doctoral thesis on thermodynamics, which unfortunately contradicted (correctly as it appeared later) a favourite principle of Marcelin Berthelot, a powerful figure in the French academic establishment. Not only did Berthelot ensure that the thesis was rejected, but he declared that Duhem would never teach in Paris. It did not take Duhem long to write another thesis of a more mathematical nature that was accepted by different examiners, but his career was permanently blighted by his clash with Berthelot.

In his first thesis Duhem has shown the usefulness of the concept of thermodynamic potential, and he deduced what is now known as the Gibbs-Duhem equation. In the following years, he consolidated his scientific reputation, working on the interaction of electric currents

---

[*] Peter Hodgson, "Pierre Duhem: Historian of the Christian Origin of Modern Science," *Month* (July 1991): 285.

and the theory of saline solutions as well as making a rigorous analysis of the foundations of thermodynamics.

His first academic appointment was to a lectureship at Lille, where he won praise for the excellence of his teaching and his devotion to his students. His lecture notes were so clearly written and logically presented that they were soon published in a series of volumes. His scientific reputation continued to grow, but because of the hostile attitude of the authorities, he was never called to Paris. Instead he was obliged to move first to Rennes and then to Bordeaux, where he spent the remainder of his life.

At that time French physics was at a low ebb, lacking the theoreticians to develop general theories and use them to unify the increasing mass of experimental data. Duhem could have been one of the leaders in this work, and indeed felt it to be his patriotic duty, but because of his banishment from Paris, he spent much of his life giving advanced lecture courses to largely empty benches.

Many of Duhem's ideas on physics were far in advance of his time and have some similarities to those of the new physics. He had always been interested in the development of scientific ideas and had read widely in the history of mechanics. He was asked to write a series of articles on this subject and meticulously followed the story from the Renaissance back to its medieval roots. During these studies he gradually became aware of the continuous development throughout the Middle Ages that culminated in the achievements of Galileo and Newton. He studied in detail the works of Leonardo da Vinci and found that da Vinci obtained many of his ideas from medieval thinkers. Gradually there opened up before Duhem's astonished eye the real story of the development of science, so different from the familiar tale of unbroken darkness between the Greeks and the Renaissance. There was, as the documents he uncovered showed, intense intellectual activity during the Middle Ages, and a leading part was played by the masters of the Parisian schools, in particular by John Buridan and Nicholas Oresme.

At that time the ideas of the nature of the world were largely derived from Aristotle, and the philosophers of the Parisian schools taught by commenting on his texts. Some of Aristotle's teaching, however, was inconsistent with the Christian faith, and the Parisian philosophers did not hesitate to differ from him whenever this seemed to be necessary. There was intense discussion on a variety of topics, notably those concerning the creation of the world and the motion of bodies. In 1277 the bishop of Paris, Etienne Tempier, found it necessary to condemn 216 philosophical propositions as contrary to the Christian belief in the creation by God of all things out of nothing. This was a turning point in the history of thought, as it channelled philosophical speculations about motion in a direction that led eventually to the destruction of Aristotelian physics, thus opening the way to modern science.

In this new intellectual climate, the 14th-century French philosopher John Buridan, considering the problem of motion, wrote that

> God, when He created the world, moved each of the celestial orbs as He pleased, and in moving them He impressed upon them impetuses which moved them without Him having to move them anymore except by the method of general influence whereby He concurs a co-agent in all things that take place.[1]

This shows a clear break with Aristotle, who required the continuing action of the mover throughout the motion. What Buridan called impetus was later refined into the concept of momentum and hence to Newton's first law of motion. Buridan's works were widely published, and his ideas became known to Leonardo da Vinci and hence to the scientists of Renaissance times.

Duhem's studies of medieval science showed him that there was a continuous scientific development throughout the Middle Ages that eventually led to the great flowering in the Renaissance. Furthermore, that development was made possible by the Christian theology of the creation of all things out of nothing by God. This tells us that matter is good and ordered and rational, presuppositions that are essential foundations of science.

---

[1] Marshall Clagett, *The Science of Mechanics in the Middle Ages* (Oxford University Press, 1959), 536.

Duhem described the transition from Greek to modern science as a gradual process:

> The demolition of Aristotelian physics was not a sudden collapse; the construction of modern physics did not take place on a terrain where nothing was left standing. From one to the other the passage takes place by a long series of partial transformations of which each pretended to retouch or enlarge some piece of the edifice without changing anything of the ensemble. But when all these modification of detail had been made the human mind perceived, as it sized up with a single look the result of all that long work, that nothing remained of the old palace and that a new palace rose in its place. Those who in the sixteenth century took stock of this substitution of one science for another were seized by a strange illusion. They imagined that this substitution was sudden and it was their work. They proclaimed that Peripatetic physics had just collapsed under their blows and that on the ruins of that physics they had built, as if by magic, the clear abode of truth. About the sincere illusion or arrogantly willful error of these men, the men of subsequent centuries were either the unsuspecting victims or sheer accomplices. The physicists of the sixteenth century were celebrated as creators to whom the world owed the Renaissance of science. They were very often but continuers and sometimes plagiarizers.

Duhem told the story of the development of science through the Middle Ages in a series of volumes: *The Evolution of Mechanics* (1973), *The Origins of Statics* (1905), the three volumes of *Studies of Leonardo da Vinci* (1906–13), and finally the ten monumental volumes of *The Structure of the World* (*Le système du monde*, 1906–59).

Duhem's demonstration of the importance of medieval thought, and particularly of the close connection between the rise of science and Christian theology, was not welcomed by the anticlerical establishment of the Third Republic or by the rationalists and secularists then dominating the historiography of science; they saw to it that his work was virtually ignored not only during his lifetime but for years after his death. The first volume of *Le système du monde*, on Greek cosmology, was warmly welcomed by the American historian George Sarton in the pages of the journal *Isis*, but the next four volumes were greeted by silence. The reason for this was simple: The second volume began with an account of astronomy in the Middle Ages, and Sarton realised the inconsistency between the work of Duhem and the secularist humanism that he was so assiduously propagating.

Tragically, Duhem died at the age of 55 in 1916, leaving the remaining five volumes of *Le système du monde* in manuscript form. There followed a long battle between Duhem's daughter Hélène, helped by a few of Duhem's friends, and Duhem's secularist enemies who were determined to prevent the publication of the second half of this magnum opus. Their delaying tactics were successful for almost four decades, and it was not until 1954 that the volumes began to be published.

In the intervening years there were many studies of medieval science by Annelise Maier, Marshall Clagett, Edward Grant, Alister Crombie, and others, and these have extended and confirmed the work of Duhem while inevitably correcting it in some details. Thus as a result of Duhem's pioneering work the study of medieval science is now well-established and can no longer be ignored.

Duhem's work as a philosopher of science is less detailed but perhaps more widely known than his historical studies. Like all working physicists, Duhem was a convinced realist. But having declared his realism in uncompromising terms, he went on to develop his philosophy of science in terms that easily give the impression that he was a positivist. His physics tended to be abstract and mathematical, without the reliance on models that is so characteristic of the Anglo-Saxon mind, and he was deeply aware that scientific theories remain open to change. Thus he is often quoted along with the throughgoing positivists who dominated the philosophy of science in the decades following his death.

In his philosophical writings he avoided both the naïve realism of the mechanists and the positivism of Mach and Comte. His books on the philosophy of science, *To Save the Phenomena: An Essay on the Idea of Physical Theory from Plato to Galileo* and *The Aim and Structure of Physical Theory*, maintain that the principal task of a scientific theory is to represent in mathematical terms the experimental laws as simply and accurately as possible, but this methodological positivism is balanced by an insistence on the need for common sense to provide assurance about external reality. Duhem believed, like all scientists, that the human mind can grasp the inner nature of the physical world, and that as physics progresses, it approaches a true and complete account of the structure of the world. Against the claim that matter is merely a fiction to account for our sensations, he insisted that the sole remedy is to 'cling with all our strength to the bedrock of common sense. Our most sublime scientific knowledge has no other foundation than the facts admitted by common sense'.

Duhem was also an accomplished artist, and a small selection of his landscapes and sketches has been published.

The work of Duhem is of great relevance today, for it shows clearly the Christian roots of modern science, thus decisively refuting the alleged incompatibility of science and Christianity still propagated by the secularist establishment. Science is an integral part of Christian culture, a lesson still to be learned even within the Christian Church. From this follows the importance of detailed and accurate scientific studies of many aspects of modern life before any moral judgements are made.

Duhem's work on the Christian origin of science has been deliberately neglected because it is unwelcome both to the heirs of the French Enlightenment and to the heirs of the Reformation. For different reasons they both wish to paint the Middle Ages as darkly as possible. His career was caught up in the battle between the secularists who fought against Christian rationality and realism and the Christians whose energies were fatally dissipated by the conflicts between liberals and conservatives. Then, as now, these two groups of Christians had one thing in common: They both ignored the importance of science in moulding our civilisation and thus failed to realise the vital importance of the work of Duhem.

On a more personal level, the life of Duhem is an example of Christian fortitude in the face of many setbacks and sorrows. The professional enmity that kept him from Paris has already been mentioned, and his work as an historian of science was ignored because its conclusions were uncongenial to the secularist-dominated establishment. In addition he lost his wife and second daughter after less than two years of happy married life. His health was never strong, and yet he wrote forty books and over 400 articles. He also found time to visit the sick and the poor. He was a devoted father, popular with his students and the children of his friends. It is appropriate that after his unexpected death in his ancestral village of Cabrespine his funeral was attended not by university dignitaries but by a throng of village folk, led by his friend the curé.

## References

### Books on Duhem

Stanley Jaki. *Uneasy Genius: The Life and Work of Pierre Duhem*. Dordrecht: Martinus Nijhoff, 1984. A detailed account of Duhem and his work as a physicist, historian, and philosopher.

———. *The Physicist as Artist: The Landscapes of Pierre Duhem*. Selected and introduced by Stanley L. Jaki. Edinburgh: Scottish Academic Press, 1988.

———. 'Science and Censorship: Hélène Duhem and the Publication of *Le système du monde*' in *The Absolute beneath the Relative, and Other Essays*. Lanham, MD: University Press of America, 1988, chapter 11.

———. *Au pays des gorilles avec Pierre Duhem (1861–1916): Un Echo de la Revolution*. Introduction by Stanley L. Jaki. Paris: Beauchesne, 1989.

———. *Scientist and Catholic: Pierre Duhem*. Front Royal, VA: Christendom Press, 1991.

### Books on Medieval Science

Marshall Clagett. *The Science of Mechanics in the Middle Ages*. Madison: University of Wisconsin Press, 1959.

A. C. Crombie. *Robert Grosseteste and the Origins of Experimental Science, 1100–1700*. Oxford: Clarendon Press, 1953. This detailed study shows that the scientific method practiced by Galileo and Newton was fully articulated, at least in its qualitative aspects, as early as the 13th century.

———. *Augustine to Galileo: The History of Science, A.D. 400–1650*. London: Falcon Press, 1952. Revised edition titled *Medieval and Early Modern Science*. Garden City, NY: Doubleday, 1959.

E. Grant. *Studies in Medieval Science and Natural Philosophy*. London: Variorum Reprints, 1981.

## *Books by Duhem on the History and Philosophy of Science*

Pierre Duhem. *L'Evolution de la mécanique.* Paris, 1903. Republished as *The Evolution of Mechanics,* translated by M. Cole, introduction by G. Oravas. Alphen aan den Rijn: Sijhoff and Noordhoff, 1980.

———. *Les origines de la statique.* Paris, 1905–6. *Etudes sur Leonardo da Vince.* 3 volumes. 1906–13. Paris: Editions Archives Contemporaires, 1984.

———. *Sauver les phenomenes.* Paris, 1908. Republished as *To Save the Phenomena: An Essay on the Idea of Physical Theory from Plato to Galileo,* translated by E. Doland and C. Maschler, with an introductory essay by Stanley L. Jaki. Chicago: University of Chicago Press, 1969.

———. *Le système du monde.* 10 volumes. Paris: Hermann et Fils, 1913–59.

———. *La theorie physique: Son objet—sa structure.* Paris, 1914. Republished as *The Aim and Structure of Physical Theory,* translated by Philip P. Wiener, with a foreword by Prince Louis de Broglie. Princeton, NJ: Princeton University Press, 1954, 1991.

———. *Medieval Cosmology: Theories of Infinity, Place, Time, Void and the Plurality of Worlds.* Edited and translated by Roger Ariew, with a foreword by Stanley L. Jaki. Chicago: University of Chicago Press, 1985. This book contains extensive extracts from volume 7 of *Le système du monde* and some sections from volumes 1, 9, and 10.

# CHAPTER 11

# Miracles

THE SUCCESS of Newtonian dynamics in accounting for the motions of the moon and the planets strongly reinforced the idea that the physical world behaves like a giant machine inexorably following fixed laws given to it on the day of creation. This immediately raises a problem about human free will and also about the action of God on the world. If indeed we as part of the physical world are simply machines, then what becomes of our humanity? Is it all, in the words of Whitehead, just the hurrying of material, endlessly, meaninglessly? Yet we know that we are free, and so in a way that we do not understand, we can make decisions and bear responsibility for them. God is also free and the Lord of nature and can act freely on the world. How can this happen without breaking the laws of nature?

How does all this affect our lives? Do we have any evidence that God cares for us? Does He give any signs of His care? Many people experience the presence of God in their lives, but this is intensely personal. Does God ever give the public signs that are called miracles? The accounts of the life of Christ and of the saints provide many examples of miracles, but these are difficult to confirm by objective criteria. Are miracles still occurring?

A miracle can be defined as an event that is inexplicable scientifically and is a sign of God's continuing presence. Science is based on the assumption of the uniformity of nature, the belief that things happen in a regular and orderly way. The same causes always produce the same effects, and science is the systematic study of these regularities. The uniformity of nature is thus a methodological presupposition and not a scientific conclusion. It cannot be proved. The fact that a causal sequence has happened a million times is no proof that it will always happen or that it is an unalterable fact of nature; it just makes it extremely improbable. The sun has been observed to rise every morning for thousands of years, and this makes it extremely likely that it will rise again tomorrow. But this is not a certainty, even in the natural order. We can imagine events such as the impact of an asteroid that would prevent it from happening. In addition, God has supreme power over nature and can suspend its laws at will or override them by more powerful forces.

The condition 'inexplicable scientifically' means that the event cannot be explained by contemporary science. How, then, do we know that it will not eventually be perfectly explicable according to new laws found by scientists in the future? Certainly if the inexplicable event happens regularly it is a suitable subject for scientific investigation. Such events usually occur in situations that are just being opened up for scientific study. This differs from cases where a familiar process is suddenly accelerated, as when, for example, a medical condition that usually takes months to heal is cured almost instantaneously.

It often happens in our experience or in the course of research that some inexplicable event occurs. We assume that it has some obscure natural explanation and try the experiment again. Eventually we succeed, and then we forget about the glitch. As anyone who has made a laboratory experiment knows all too well, all sorts of things mysteriously go wrong, and it requires great persistence finally to get the apparatus to work as planned. We certainly do not call such difficulties miracles. For an event to be declared a miracle, it has to be identified as a sign from God. By its nature a sign has to be recognised, and it can be recognised only by a prepared mind, that is, by a believer in God's creative power. It is no criticism of a particular person if he does not recognise a miracle. Thus an X-ray film is a sign that conveys information about our state of health, but it can be interpreted only by a trained radiographer with years of experience.

As an example, Alexis Carrel was an agnostic medical doctor. He was open-minded enough to go to Lourdes to investigate the cures alleged to take place there. While at Lourdes he observed the almost instantaneous cure of a girl who was dying of acute peritonitis. He did not call it a miracle; as a scientist he simply recorded the event and concluded that such cures can take place in response to prayer. He wrote that they are 'stubborn, irreducible facts, which must be taken into account'. As a result he was no longer welcome in the agnostic and anticlerical medical establishment at Lyons and was forced to leave France. He joined the Rockefeller Institute for medical research in the United States, where his work on heart surgery led to the award of the Nobel Prize, and, incidentally, saved my own life many decades later. A few years before he died, Carrel returned to the faith of his childhood; remarkably, this happened soon after the death from natural causes of the girl he had seen cured.

The Church has established extremely strict criteria that must be satisfied before a miracle is confirmed. Cases considered must be medical conditions that are physical and not psychological. The Medical Bureau at Lourdes keeps detailed records, and doctors of all faiths—or of no faith—are welcome to examine the patients. Most cases are rejected at an early stage because the evidence is not sufficient. It is only when the medical doctors have certified that there is no medical explanation that the Church will set up a committee to consider the possibility that it is a miracle. Nearly all modern miracles involve cures of diseases and other medical conditions. An exception is provided by the phenomenon of the sun at Fatima, which is particularly interesting to physicists, although it has not been declared a miracle. This has recently been subjected to detailed study and analysis by the priest-physicist Stanley Jaki in his book *God and the Sun at Fatima*. Although this phenomenon was unprecedented and seen by a large crowd of witnesses, it cannot be proved that it was not an extremely rare meteorological phenomenon. The argument that it was indeed a miracle rests on the prediction, many months in advance, that it would take place on that particular day. As a result, tens of thousands of people came to see what would happen, many of them expecting or hoping that nothing would happen. Furthermore, it was not a pointless display of divine power; it had a critical effect on the political situation in Portugal and hence on the subsequent history to Europe.

Most people nowadays reject miracles out of hand and refuse to look at the evidence. They consider anyone who even admits the possibility of miracles as credulous and naïve. However, it is they who are credulous by accepting that the uniformity of nature is an established truth that always holds without exception. They laugh at the Aristotelian philosophers who refused to look through Galileo's telescope, and yet they are behaving in just the same way by refusing even to examine the evidence for miracles. In both cases the underlying thought is the same: Even to look at the evidence implies recognition of the possibility that it might force them to change their minds, and they are afraid that this might happen.

## CHAPTER 12

# Can Physics Contradict the Truths of Faith?

ONE OFTEN HEARS arguments based on physics that purport to throw doubt on some aspect of religious belief. For example, it is argued that our free will is contrary to the law of conservation of energy or that the latest cosmological theory removes the need for a Creator.

To see what lies behind these arguments, we must examine what exactly is proved by physical science and what is not. The aim of the physicist is to reveal in ever more detail the structure and motions of the physical world. To do this he makes careful observations and systematic experiments and then tries to express his results as simply as possible by empirical laws. For example, he may decide to study the way a bar of iron expands when it is heated. He therefore makes careful measurements of the length of the bar at various temperatures. He plots his results on a graph of length against temperature and discovers that within the limits of the experimental uncertainties it is a straight line. It is therefore easy to write down a mathematical formula that gives the length of the bar as a function of temperature with a coefficient of expansion obtained from the slope of the line. This is an empirical law. He may then repeat the experiment for other metals and see if he can find a relation between the coefficient of expansion of each metal with some other characteristic of the metal, such as its density or atomic weight. If he succeeds in this, he can combine his results into a more general formula.

Physicists are always trying to unify wide ranges of phenomena under general laws. For example, in the 19th century there was great interest in the phenomena of electricity and magnetism. Volta found a way to generate an electric current, and this allowed Ohm and Ampere and Faraday and many others to make electrical experiments. They found that there was an intimate relation between electricity and magnetism. This enabled Maxwell to formulate his four equations that describe all electromagnetic phenomena to high accuracy.

The vital question concerns the status of these equations. Are they a true and exact description of reality or just the best approximation we have so far? Certainly they are not like the simple empirical laws already mentioned, which must be accepted as true. More precisely, are they true ontologically or empirically? We know that it would be possible to make a minute change in the formulae that would not affect the agreement with experiment. We cannot exclude the possibility that another set of equations will one day be found that also agrees with the experiment. Such considerations force us to conclude that the equations are empirical.

This conclusion is reinforced when we reflect that Newton's laws of motion were extremely successful but were eventually shown to be inadequate for very high velocities and so were replaced by Einstein's relativistic laws. Physicists believe that the universe is made in a definite way and that our theories approach more and more closely to an exact description of that reality, but they also believe that we can never know whether we have achieved that objective. We can always imagine that however well our theories describe all the present experimental data, further experiments may reveal that in more extreme conditions they may prove inadequate, and so they must be replaced by a more accurate theory.

Thus we can never say that our physical theories are either true or false; they are not statements about ultimate reality but about our provisional attempts to describe reality. From this it follows immediately that they are of a different character from the truths of religion, and so can neither confirm nor deny them.

# CHAPTER 13

# Charles A. Coulson: Scientist and Man of Faith, 1910–1974

CHARLES COULSON combined a brilliant career as professor of mathematics and theoretical chemistry with a deep and humble Christian faith. He wrote widely on science and faith, and these writings have had a wide and lasting influence.

He went up to Cambridge in 1928 and soon came under the influence of several scientists who were also practising Christians, in particular Arthur Eddington the cosmologist, Charles Raven the naturalist, and Alex Wood the physicist. Coulson gave the Alex Wood Memorial Lecture in 1953. In it he recalled that when he was reading mathematics in Cambridge he was puzzled to know to what extent he should allow his love for his subject to dominate his future life.

> The two competing possibilities were represented in my mind by two people—one was a most distinguished mathematician with a world-wide reputation; he was a symbol of a life so wholly devoted to academic study that it merited the epitaph "this man decided to know, and not to live". The other was Alex Wood, symbol for me then, as now, of the life of a man whose service to God lies not only through his learning, but no less through his social conscience, his power among people, his simple Christian affection. If, in the end, my puzzle was solved, it was because this second man was so attractive that I felt that I wanted to be a bit like him.'[1]

---

[1] 'Fellowship of Reconciliation', Alex Wood Memorial Lecture, 1953.

Coulson followed this ideal so faithfully that what he wrote of Alex Wood describes his own life and influence. From his first year in Cambridge, when he became involved in a Methodist group movement, his Christian faith was the driving force of his life.

There [were] some ten of us and together we sought for God and together we found Him. I learnt for the first time in my life that God was my friend. . . . God became real to me—utterly real—I knew Him and could talk with Him as I had never imagined it possible before. And these prayers . . . were the most glorious moments of the day. Life had a purpose and that purpose coloured everything.

This quotation is from a sermon Coulson preached in 1931, and the faith based on religious experience never left him.

The group members were very conscious of the need to be intellectually honest, and as many of them were scientists, they were bound to consider the relationship between their science and their religion.

His first and most fundamental area of concern was therefore the relation of science and Christian belief, and his thinking is summed up in a book with that title. He knew from his own experience the truth of science and of his Christian faith, and his life exemplified their harmony.

His scientific research showed him 'more and more of the austerity of its discipline, and its quite astonishing power of building up a coherent picture of the universe in which we live. There was a strength, there was a pattern, there was even grandeur in this—surely there must be truth also.'[2]

He knew from the inside the excitement, the sense of achievement, and the power of science and recognised that it had become 'the cohesive force in modern society, the ground on which may be built a secure way of life for man and for communities'.[3] Such is the prestige of science that 'if we are to restore faith to man, it will be through science'.[4]

---

[2] 'The Unity of Science and Faith', *Christianity in an Age of Science* (Ottawa: Canadian Broadcasting Corporation), 41.

[3] *Science and Christian Belief* (London and Glasgow: Fontana Books, Wm. Collins Sons & Co., 1971), 20.

[4] Ibid., 21.

Many Christians 'cannot face the implications of the new knowledge, and insist on some sort of nostalgic return to things as they were, but this is an attitude born of fear, and almost entirely unproductive'.[5] The only hope for the Christian, as for the scientist, is to 'follow uncompromisingly wherever we are led, into whatever abyss or on to whatever height, and accept whatever we may meet upon the way'.[6]

There must be no competition between science and religion for areas of human experience. It is particularly dangerous to seek God in the ever-contradicting areas as yet unexplained by science, a line of thought summed up in the phrase 'God of the gaps'. 'When we come to the scientifically unknown, the correct policy is not to rejoice because we have found God; it is to become better scientists, and to think a bit more deeply until we can devise some model, or some concept, that will bring the previous unknown into the pattern of the known.'[7] 'God must be found within the known, and not the unknown.'[8]

There was for Coulson no separation of his life into two compartments, the scientific and the Christian. 'If the glory of God does not shine through science, if the work of science cannot be seen as God's work, then, as a scientist, I am involved in a duality of experience which will ultimately become quite intolerable.'[9] The scientist is studying God's world, and this is seen in science itself: 'I want to be able to look at science, its methods, its presuppositions, its basis, its splendid successes and its austere discipline; and then I want to be able to say: Here is God revealing Himself for those with eyes to see.'[10]

In order to see this more clearly, 'the scientist must look at the manner of the enquiry, the presuppositions which inform it, the corporate nature which it shares and his own human reactions and response to what he finds within it'.[11] In this way, 'science is recognised

[5] Ibid., 26.

[6] Ibid., 29.

[7] 'Science and Religion: A Changing Relationship', Rede Lecture, 1954. (Cambridge: Cambridge University Press, [1955]), 7.

[8] *Science and Christian Belief*, 3.

[9] Ibid., 45.

[10] Ibid., 44.

[11] 'Science and the Idea of God', 11th Arthur Stanley Eddington Memorial Lecture, 1958 (Cambridge: Cambridge University Press, 1958), 27.

as one of the languages in which God is revealed, and the work of scientists is seen as God's work'.[12]

Science depends on certain basic convictions, and without these it could never have begun.

> Think for a moment of some of the attitudes of mind with which any scientist comes to his search: there is honesty, integrity and hope: there is enthusiasm, for no one ever yet began an experiment without an element of passion: there is an identification of himself with the experiment, a partisan character about his secret hope for its conclusion which not even an adverse result can wholly extinguish: there is a humility before a created order of things, which is to be received and studied: there is a singleness of mind about the search which reveals what the scientist himself may often hesitate to confess, that he does what he does because it seems exciting and it somehow fulfills a deep part of his very being: there is cooperation with his fellows, both in the same laboratory and across the seven seas: there is patience, akin to that which kept Mme Curie at her self-imposed task of purifying eight tons of pitchblende to extract the few odd milligrams of radium: above all there is judgement— judgement as to what constitutes worth-while research: judgement as to what is fit and suitable for publication. . . . Science could not exist, and certainly is not practised, without all these qualities. They build the ethos and tradition which every scientist must accept and to which he must conform.[13]

An examination of scientific method thus shows that 'science is only possible in a community where certain religious views are widely held'.[14] 'However little its followers may recognise this, science is one of the ways in which God is revealed'.[15] 'The scientist's longing for truth, his passion to get to the root of things, his moments of doubt no less than his moments of illumination, are all essentially religious in character'.[16]

---

[12] 'Science and Religion', 22.
[13] *Science and Christian Belief,* 72.
[14] Ibid., 80.
[15] Ibid., 45.
[16] 'Science and the Idea of God', 38.

Thus 'science is an essentially religious activity'[17] as indeed is to be expected as it was 'born and cradled in the Christian faith'.[18]

> In its methods of working, in its dependence upon the assumption of a spiritual wholeness about life, in its insistence upon the richness and variety of experience, and the interrelatedness of all things within the role of a person, the changing pattern of science has come back to something more like harmony with the Christian faith: but in the new harmony there are new notes which would never have sounded but for the patience, the integrity, the creative imagination of men of science.[19]

The fusion of Christian faith and scientific research formed a centre from which Coulson's activity and thought radiated in many directions. From his Cambridge days he immersed himself in a wide range of activities outside his scientific work. In the 1930s he served on committees of the Fellowship of Reconciliation and the Methodist Peace Fellowship and was accepted as a conscientious objector during the war. In the 1950s he joined the Campaign for Nuclear Disarmament and wrote widely on the hazards of nuclear weapons and the potential blessings of the peaceful applications of atomic power. When from 1959 to 1960 he was president of the Methodist Conference, his particular contribution was that he, a scientist and an academic, was able to demonstrate the complementary nature of science and religion when dealing with the problems of the world. He carried this to the World Council of Churches, for which he served on the Central Committee from 1962 to 1968, and to Oxfam, of which he was chairman from 1965 to 1971.

His activity extended to students and colleagues overseas, indeed to all, from the distinguished to the ordinary, to whom he could give some of his overflowing attention. By his actions he showed that he knew that 'the Christian has a particular responsibility. First, not to deny the new knowledge or seek to evade the decisions that it brings, but soberly to welcome both as a gift from God; second, to insist that

---

[17] *Science and Christian Belief,* 45.
[18] 'Science and the Idea of God', 7.
[19] 'Science and Religion', 34.

all the applications of this knowledge be considered only in the light of that understanding which we have in the Lord Jesus Christ'.[20]

He lectured widely, and many of his lectures have been published almost as he gave them. He spoke from the heart, always aiming to open the eyes of his hearers to the boundless wonder of the world of science and the insights and responsibilities of the Christian. He wanted them to 'taste and see' and brought to his lectures a vivid immediacy by numerous quotations and stories from his vast reading. He had neither the time nor the inclination for detailed philosophical arguments.

He saw very clearly the vast potentialities and dangers of the widespread application of science and was acutely conscious that science could be developed wisely only in a Christian context. Yet Christians on the whole are not conscious of their responsibilities. 'It is a tragedy to have to confess that if I wanted to be among a group of people who would feel in their bones a responsibility for what is going on around them, I should not choose a church audience; I should choose a scientific one'.[21] He saw it as his task to alert his fellow Christians to the dangers and to spur them into action. This formed the theme of his Beckley Social Service Lecture in 1960, later published as *Science, Technology and the Christian*. In these lectures and on many other occasions he described the problems of the world today, problems that have sometimes been magnified, sometimes almost solved, by the applications of science. So many people in the world lack the basic necessities of life. They do not have enough to eat, they live in hovels, and they are ravaged by disease. In science we have the means to end this misery; from whence will come the will? In a lecture entitled 'Science and Religion,' he urged that

> [I]f we are to make the most of opportunities which a time like this requires of us, and which are potentially within our grasp, it will be by bringing together these two large fields of action and response to the human spirit, not in conflict but in cooperation. As Einstein said, 'Science without religion is blind'—for example, it cannot see

---

[20] 'Some Problems of the Atomic Age', second Scott Lidget Memorial Lecture, 1957 (Norwich, UK: Epworth Press, [1957]), 35.

[21] 'Responsibility', second Tawney Memorial Lecture, 21.

what needs to be done, or fill people with the urgent sense that they must do something about it.

And then he went on: 'Religion without science is lame': good intentions alone will not get you very far in feeding the hungry multi-tudes of India. If we can bring these two movements of the human spirit together, and forget about the growing pains which led to the freedom of scientists to have their own concepts and religious theirs, the combination will constitute one of the very best possible tools for making the earth something like what, in our better moments, we know it ought to be.[22]

He knew very well the great potentialities and dangers of atomic energy for the future of mankind, and like so many scientists after the war, he saw it as his social duty to do all in his power to tell people of the choice before us. He lectured to all types of audiences, from schools to learned conferences, on the hazards of atomic weapons and the blessings of atomic power and its peaceful applications.

The development of atomic weapons did not pose any new moral problems to him; rather it confirmed his belief that all war is immoral. Indeed, he thought that on balance the advent of atomic weapons might even help peace, for it underlines the fundamental issue of the present state of our civilisation, that we are inescapably bound together, that it is one world—or none. After the war, he was invited several times to join teams working on the development of nuclear reactors because, in the course of his normal research, he had come to know more than anyone else about certain properties of graphite. But he knew that 'they want this knowledge in order that they may perfect the means of destruction',[23] so he declined all the invitations and, in addition, changed his research interests.

He was filled with a sense of urgency when he saw that 'through the efforts of scientists mankind has now acquired almost unlimited power. Do we know how to use it rightly? I am not sure. We have devised not one, but several, ways in which we can destroy one another

---

[22] *Proceedings of the Royal Institution of Great Britain* 41 (1967): 492.
[23] *The Scientists' Responsibility in Society* (Edinburgh: Heriot-Watt University, 1970), 26.

from off the face of the earth. Most of us in the scientific movement are greatly troubled'.[24] But

> not until the power conferred by our knowledge has been recog-
> nised as God's gift, enabling His children to grow up into fully
> developed men and women; not until man's new independence is
> seen to be but the liberty of the children of God; not until man's
> patient observation of the world around [him] has led him on to
> awe and then to worship; not until our science has shown us with
> what rich lustre the heavens declare the glory of God and the firma-
> ment shows his handwork; not until then can human faith be as it
> was meant to be, nor human life fulfill its proper destiny; so we
> shall see how all things are summed up in Christ, both things on
> earth and things in heaven; and our hearts be so astonished at the
> splendour of God's creation that they grasp eternity in a moment of
> time, and are lost in wonder, love and praise.[25]

## Reference

Charles A. Coulson. *Epworth Review* (May 1975): 19.

---

[24] *Advancement of Science* (1954), 11: 331.
[25] Ibid., 332.

# CHAPTER 14

# Louis Leprince-Ringuet, 1901–2000

LOUIS LEPRINCE-RINGUET was one of the leading French scientists for much of the 20th century. He graduated in 1920 in engineering and spent several years laying and servicing submarine cables. In 1929 he decided to devote his energies to research and joined the laboratory of Maurice de Broglie, brother of the more famous Louis de Broglie. There he designed detectors of nuclear radiations and worked with Pierre Auger on cosmic rays in the early 1930s.

At that time, little was known about the cosmic rays. Their intensity increased with altitude, indicating that they come from outer space, but their nature was unknown. In order to find out whether they consisted of charged or neutral particles, Leprince-Ringuet and Auger travelled by ship from Hamburg to Buenos Aires and measured the intensity of the cosmic radiation throughout the voyage. They found that the intensity varied with latitude, indicating that the particles are charged and are therefore deflected by the earth's magnetic field. If they had been neutral, the intensity would have remained the same throughout the voyage.

Leprince-Ringuet continued his work on cosmic radiation by studying the rays on mountains, where they are more intense, and also during balloon flights. In 1936 he became a professor at the Ecole Polytechnique in Paris and headed a laboratory devoted to cosmic ray research.

After the war, cosmic ray research became a very active field, involving many scientists worldwide. Cosmic rays were shown to consist of protons and other heavier nuclei of very high energy. These collide with nuclei high in the atmosphere and produce showers of short-lived particles called mesons and hyperons. A historic conference was held in 1953 in Bagneres-de-Bigorre in the south of France to discuss and evaluate these new results. It was there that I met Leprince-Ringuet; he was naturally one of the leading participants in the discussions, but he also attended Mass daily.

At that time most of the knowledge of the new unstable elementary particles like mesons and hyperons had been attained by studies of cosmic radiation. At that time more and more powerful accelerators were being built, able to produce copious beams of particles of well-defined energies. It soon became clear that further studies of these particles could best be obtained from the accelerators and not from cosmic radiation. This was highlighted by Leprince-Ringuet's final speech at the conference.

As a result, Leprince-Ringuet reorientated his research and supported the construction of a new, powerful proton synchrotron at the European Centre for Nuclear Research (CERN) in Geneva. He also organised the construction of two large bubble chambers, one of hydrogen and one of helium, that were used to detect the interaction produced by the particles coming from the new accelerator.

He strongly supported the foundation of CERN as a cooperative venture between twelve countries and for many years served as chairman of its scientific policy committee. He was a member of the French Academy of Sciences and of the French Atomic Energy Commission and was elected to the French Academy in 1966.

In a life spanning almost the whole of the 20th century, Louis Leprince-Ringuet was a scientist of the highest distinction who made many important discoveries and inspired generations of physicists.

# CHAPTER 15

# Fred Hoyle,
# 1915–2001

FRED HOYLE was one of the most distinguished astronomers of the 20th century. In 1958, together with William Fowler, he identified the nuclear reactions in the interior of stars that built up the nuclei of the chemical elements heavier than the original hydrogen. He showed, in other words, that we are all made of star dust.

He also developed theories of star formation and planet condensation. He was Plumian Professor of Astronomy at Cambridge from 1958 to 1972, was president of the Royal Astronomical Society from 1971 to 1973, and received numerous scientific distinctions. He wrote many books, including *Frontiers of Astronomy* (1955), *Star Formation* (1963), *Galaxies, Nuclei and Quasars* (1965), *The Relation of Physics and Cosmology* (1973), and *The Cosmology of the Solar System* (1978). In spite of his great scientific distinction, he was better known to the general public through his advocacy of unpopular theories and his wide range of popular writings.

He admitted that he had an aesthetic bias against what he mockingly called the Big Bang theory, a name that stuck. As an alternative, he proposed, together with Bondi and Gold, the Steady State theory, the idea that, averaged over space and time, the universe always has the same large-scale characteristics. To take account of the known recession of the galaxies, they postulated the spontaneous appearance of sufficient hydrogen atoms to keep the average density the same.

The rate of appearance was far below anything that could be detected experimentally.

Underlying this scientific controversy was the feeling that the Big Bang theory supported the idea of a creation by God at a certain instant of time, an idea abhorrent to the secularism of Hoyle and his colleagues. It is now clear that this is a double confusion.

Science by its very nature can never prove such an absolute beginning, and Creation in the theological sense means the continual keeping in existence rather than a temporal beginning. Thus, the universe would still need a Creator even if it existed from all eternity, although we know from revelation that it had a temporal beginning. The scientist who first proposed the Big Bang theory, Georges Lemaitre, a Belgian Catholic priest, was quite clear about this and was totally opposed to the use of the theory to support belief in creation.

The Steady State theory was a genuine scientific theory, but it is now believed to be disproved by galaxy counts and by the discovery of microwave background radiation.

Hoyle, together with his colleague Chandra Wickramasinghe, caused furious controversy by claiming that sunspots cause flu epidemics, that Darwin's theory of evolution by natural selection is wrong, that evolution occurs because mutating life-forms fall on the earth from space, and that the skeleton of Archaeopteryx, an intermediate between a reptile and a bird and one of the pieces of evidence favouring evolution, is a fake. They maintained that space is full of viruses that cause not only flu but also AIDS and Legionnaire's disease and that this was all arranged by a superintelligent alien civilisation. Hoyle was a prolific writer of science fiction, particularly *The Black Cloud* (1957), *A for Andromeda* (1962), and a children's play, *Rockets in Ursa Major* (1962). Together with his son Geoffrey he wrote *Common Sense and Nuclear Energy* (1979), a well-argued case for nuclear power.

Hoyle's atheism received a severe shock when he discovered the amazing properties of the nuclei of beryllium and oxygen, which conspire to make possible the formation of the nucleus of carbon, on which all life depends. This is described in his autobiography, *Home Is Where the Wind Blows* (1994), which also gives an account of his scientific work and controversies. In later life his views seemed to have mellowed somewhat, and now he knows the truth at last.

# CHAPTER 16

# Wilhelm Roentgen: Discoverer of X-Rays, 1845–1923

ON 9 NOVEMBER 1895, Professor Wilhelm Roentgen of the University of Wurzburg was studying the cathode rays that are emitted when an electric current is passed through an evacuated tube. Professor J. J. Thomson of Cambridge had recently shown that the cathode rays are beams of electrons, and many physicists were trying to find out more about them.

Roentgen's experiments were carried out in a darkened room, and as the current passed through the tube he was surprised to see some nearby crystals fluoresce brightly. This could not be due to the cathode rays because the tube was covered by black paper, thick enough to stop the electrons. He moved the crystals farther away from the tube, and still they fluoresced. The only possible explanation was that some unknown radiation, of great penetrating power, was emitted from the cathode. Since he did not know what the rays were, Roentgen called them X-rays.

He was alone when he made this discovery, and he kept it quiet while he thoroughly checked his observations. In a few weeks of intense activity, he determined many of the properties of X-rays. He found that they easily penetrate paper, wood, cloth, and many metals, though more easily through light metals than through heavy metals. He thought that they should also pass through flesh, and he showed this by photographing a hand. The rays passed more easily through the flesh than they did through the bones, and so the photograph showed the skeleton of the hand.

Roentgen presented a preliminary report of his discovery to the Physical and Medical Society of Wurzburg on 28 December 1895. He described his apparatus and said that his investigations showed that many substances fluoresce when irradiated by X-rays, and he tabulated the penetrabilities of the rays through several metals. He reported that the intensity of X-rays diminishes as the square of the distance from the source. Unlike the cathode rays, X-rays are not deflected by a magnetic field, and he failed to find any evidence that they can be diffracted or reflected or that they can interfere. He also suggested that they are produced when the cathode rays hit the walls of the discharge tube.

This report was printed early in January 1896 and was soon translated into many languages. It produced an international sensation, and physicists in many countries soon confirmed the discovery. Some people were sceptical at first but were soon convinced by the astonishing photographs of objects inside opaque boxes—and most of all by the skeletal hands. Eager journalists waxed lyrical about the sensational implications of the discovery. One of them, Mr H. J. W. Dam of *McClure's Magazine*, interviewed Roentgen and wrote what is probably the fullest and most accurate account of the discovery. Others drew freely on their imaginations. Cartoonists had a field day comparing photographs of social events with the pictures that they imagined could be taken with X-rays. Ladies feared what the rays might reveal, and fraudsters advertised X-ray-proof corsets.

This was the first time that a scientific discovery had received such publicity, and Roentgen became an international celebrity overnight. The features of the reception, the good and bad journalism, the inflated claims and commercial exploitation are very similar to what happens today, over 100 years later.

The medical applications of X-rays were immediately recognised, and soon X-rays were being widely used to reveal bone fractures and foreign bodies, such as bullets, needles, and lead shot. This information was of great value to surgeons, as it showed them exactly where to operate. However, many early X-ray pioneers suffered severe burns and loss of hair from repeated irradiations, and it was realised that shielding is essential to protect the operators of X-ray equipment. Even the loss of hair was exploited by charlatans, who, oblivious to the dangers, advertised that X-rays could remove unwanted hair.

Roentgen was a quiet, retiring man interested only in continuing his research and was much dismayed when he found himself thrust into the glare of publicity. He seldom gave public lectures or interviews and declined almost all the honours offered to him. He made an exception for the Nobel Prize, and his was the first awarded for physics. He could have made a vast fortune by patenting his discovery, but he refused to do so, believing that it is the duty of a scientist to make his discoveries freely available to all. He quietly continued his researches and published the results from time to time when available.

Within a short time, there were hundreds of Roentgenologists (as they were called) around the world, studying X-rays and their applications, and they published their results in thousands of books and papers. Soon after the discovery, X-rays were often called roentgen rays, but this later fell into disuse. Roentgen is, however, commemorated by the unit of radiation dose named after him.

Unlike Roentgen himself, many people did seek to profit from the rays. Quite legitimately, medical practitioners charged for making X-ray photographs. Others advertised that they could remove unwanted hair and absconded with their clients' money when the results were not in accord with expectations. The optimism of the journalists stimulated bizarre requests: One man asked for his opera glasses to be fitted with X-rays, and another asked for a pound of X-rays to be sent to him by return of post. Another claimed to have changed ordinary metal to gold with X-rays.

The idea of all-penetrating rays fired the imaginations of enthusiasts for spiritualism, soul photography, fortune-telling, and telepathy. Others hoped that it would render vivisection superfluous. Proponents of the temperance movement hoped that X-rays would promote their cause by showing the steady deterioration of the bodies of drinkers. It was claimed that Roentgen's discovery corroborates St Paul's doctrine of the spiritual body existing in man. Others claimed to produce an impression on a photographic plate by gazing at it in the

dark. Dr Baraduc described the marvellous possibilities of soul photography, claiming that photographs could be produced by thought
transmission over large distances. These and many other fantasies are
not unlike some of those inspired nowadays by the so-called mysteries
of the quantum world. They were soon forgotten.

At the time of Roentgen's discovery, many physicists had been
studying cathode rays for several years, and they all had the means to
discover the X-ray. Theoreticians had suggested that such rays might
exist, and they were certainly observed many times before 1896. It
was Roentgen's genius to recognise the importance of that first observation and to follow up on it with single-minded dedication. This
opportunity came to him because of the skill acquired during many
years of careful experimentation that would have earned him an hon-
oured place in the history of physics even had he never discovered the
X-ray. Experiments in physics are made for a particular purpose, and
the mind of the physicist is concentrated on that purpose. If an unexpected effect is observed, it may easily be brushed aside as irrelevant.
This has often happened in physics. For example, nuclear fission was
probably observed many times before it was recognised in 1939; many
scientists were able to confirm the discovery within a few hours. It is
only the exceptional physicist who can recognise the importance of
the unexpected and follow it to its conclusion.

The discovery of X-rays by Roentgen thus serves to illustrate
many facets of scientific research and the way it is received by the public. The experiment was relatively easy to do, but only a genius could
see the implications of that chance observation. It was treated respon-
sibly by a few journalists and irresponsibly by most. Numerous frauds,
fools, and tricksters tried to make money on it or to use it to enhance
their fantasies. X-rays have proved extremely beneficial but, like so
many benefits of science, have to be handled with care if disaster is to
be avoided.

# CHAPTER 17

# Science in Muslim Countries

IN HIS RECENT lecture Lord Carey, the former archbishop of Canterbury, remarked that 'it is sad to relate that no great invention has come for many hundreds of years from Muslim countries'. This is in sharp contrast to the whole development of modern science, from Newton onward, that took place in Europe and has spread throughout the world.

Certainly there are now many universities in Muslim countries, with well-equipped scientific departments, but nevertheless the standard of their work is disappointing. Muslim countries contain one-fifth of the world population, more than the United States, western Europe, and Japan combined. The fifty-seven nations in the Muslim world invest less than 0.2% of their combined GNP in research and development, so it is not surprising that most of them remain poor and underdeveloped.

The size of the Muslim scientific community is very small, and the papers written by the scientists and engineers account for just 2% of the world total. With one or two exceptions, there are no great university departments or world-calibre research institutes. There are fewer physicists in all nineteen universities in Pakistan than in Imperial College of the University of London. The science that exists in the Muslim world is largely imported from the West. There are some excellent Muslim scientists, but most of them have been trained in the West. There is rather little highly original science in Muslim countries. The most famous contemporary Muslim scientist, Abdus Salam, who won the Nobel Prize for his work in elementary particle physics, described the situation as 'abysmal'. He was born in Lahore and spent many years in Cambridge. Muslims have readily accepted the technology of the West and have the means to pay for it, but in the realm of pure science they lag behind, as they have done for centuries.

Why is this so? Over a millennium ago, from the 8th to the 14th century, Muslim science flourished. There were astronomical observatories from Cordoba to Baghdad and many schools of mathematics, physics, chemistry, and medicine. Words like 'algebra' and 'alchemy' serve to remind us of these achievements. In the first half of that period, Muslim science led the world, and yet in the second half it declined, while in the West science surged ahead. The Muslim world had about a 500-year head start in science and technology, and yet it faded away. The Muslim leaders were well aware of what was happening, but they were unable to prevent it. We may reflect on how different the course of history would have been had the Muslims led the way to modern science.

Many reasons have been suggested for this astonishing failure, ranging from the sociological to the theological. Perhaps the authoritarian structure of Muslim society made it less likely that there would be groups of scholars, such as existed in Western universities, who put forward new ideas and discussed them freely. Perhaps it was the literal interpretation of the Koran that discouraged new ideas.

There were indeed three main schools of Muslim philosophers: One school held that the Koran should be interpreted literally, another held that reason is paramount in science, and the third combined elements of both schools. After discussions extending over centuries, it was the first school that achieved dominance.

These questions are still the subject of intense discussion, and the results may show how the science in Muslim countries can be brought up to the level existing in the West.

# PART III
# Nuclear Physics

# CHAPTER 18

# Nuclear Power, Energy, and the Environment*

## The Sleeping Volcano

A FEW YEARS ago I read a beautifully written story called *The Violins of St Jacques*.[1] It was about life on an idyllic volcanic Caribbean island. The carefree islanders enjoyed themselves in the tropical sunshine, and they loved parties. At one of these parties they were dancing the night away to the music of the violins. During an interval one or two of the dancers, taking a stroll in the garden, noticed signs of activity in the long-dormant volcano: just a distant rumble and a faint red glow in the sky. Then the violins struck up the next tune, and the dancing resumed. The dancers took more notice when the streams of red-hot lava started to flow down the mountain, and soon they were running toward the harbour to take to the boats. It was too late. The volcano exploded, and the next morning the whole island had vanished beneath the waves. It is said that on a quiet day it is still possible, when sailing over the place where the island had been, to hear the sound of the violins.

As a general rule, we never rouse ourselves to take effective action until it is too late. The signs of possible impending disaster may appear from time to time, but we are busy with so many important things

---

* Peter Hodgson, "Nuclear Power, Energy, and the Environment," *St. Austin Review* (October 2001): 18.

[1] *The Violins of Saint-Jacques* by Patrick Leigh Fermor (London: John Murray, 1953).

that we never get around to doing anything about it. The newspaper headlines are mostly devoted to passing trivialities and ignore the underlying trends that will eventually dominate our future.

One of these trends concerns our energy supply. We all expect, as a matter of course, that when we turn on the switch the light will come on and that there will always be a plentiful supply of affordable fuel. As the recent revolt over fuel prices showed, we are outraged when the prices rise yet again. We can hardly blame the government for the weather, but we cannot help noticing that here and elsewhere weather seems to be changing for the worse. There are disastrous floods not only in Mozambique and Venezuela but also here in Britain. The last few years have been among the warmest in the century. It may of course be just a series of coincidences, and anyway, there is not much we can do about it. Let the violins play on.

There are indeed many things that are uncertain, but others can be studied. We can look at the various sources of our energy supply and estimate how long they are likely to last. The results are not reassuring. Throughout the last century we have come to rely more and more on oil and the associated natural gas for our energy. It is a convenient and efficient source of heat, and it is relatively easy to extract from the ground and to transport large distances to where it is needed. But how long will it last? An oil well may last about thirty years, but eventually it runs dry. The oil companies are continually searching for new oil fields, but the rate of new discoveries is slowing down. It is expected that world oil production will reach a peak in a few decades and will then start to decline.

This will not happen suddenly. As the oil becomes scarcer, the price will increase and production will decline. Countries with their own oil wells will be in a strong position, and this could lead to international tensions. Since about two-thirds of world oil reserves are in the Middle East, that area will continue to be rather sensitive.

We can always fall back on coal, which still supplies much of our energy. That will last much longer than oil, probably several hundred years. But eventually the deposits that can be worked economically will be gone. It is quite possible that these estimates for the lifetime of our oil and coal reserves will turn out to be pessimistic, and it can be argued that in any case the problem of energy supplies will not become acute for a long time. But before we allow ourselves to become complacent, we have to consider pollution and climate change.

## Pollution and Climate Change

At the present rate of consumption, world oil supplies are predicted to last about sixty years. Coal, as we have discussed, will last for several hundred years. In addition, wood, which is still extensively used in many developing countries, will remain available. So it looks as if the world has enough energy for the foreseeable future.

However, all of these energy sources rely on the burning of carbon, which combines with the oxygen in the air to form carbon dioxide, emitting heat in the process. In addition, impurities in the fuel lead to the formation of many poisonous gases, which are also emitted into the atmosphere. Foremost among these are sulphur dioxide and the oxides of nitrogen. Each year, the typical coal power station emits into the atmosphere 11,000,000 tons of carbon dioxide, 16,000 tons of sulphur dioxide, 29,000 tons of nitrous oxide, 1,000 tons of dust, and smaller amounts of a whole range of chemicals, such as aluminium, calcium, potassium, titanium, and arsenic. In addition, it creates over 1,000,000 tons of ash, 500,000 tons of gypsum, and 21,000 tons of sludge. This is not particularly hazardous, but it all has to be gotten rid of. Often it is dumped into estuaries or the sea, where it destroys the habitat of the marine life.

Over the years, these poisons poured into the atmosphere have caused many noticeable effects. They are washed down as acid rain, polluting lakes and rivers and causing the fishes to die. Over large areas in central Europe and North America the trees have started to die. These are definite observable effects. In addition, our own health is not improved by this pollution of the air we breathe. Much of the pollution is caused by factories, which are now more strictly controlled, but if we want to eliminate it entirely then carbon-burning power stations must be replaced by other energy sources.

This course of action is supported by the possibility that the additional carbon dioxide in the atmosphere is responsible for the changes in the climate. This is by no means certain, and to be sure, we have to prove that the climate really is changing and that this is due to the extra carbon dioxide in the atmosphere.

By climate we mean the weather, the sun and the rain, temperature and humidity, wind and frost, fog and snow. These are always changing from one day to the next, and from year to year. It is notoriously difficult to establish the presence of an underlying trend in a quantity that is fluctuating. Furthermore, the short-term fluctuations are superposed on long-term fluctuations, so that even if we can establish the presence of an underlying trend, we can never be sure how long it will persist. There have been ice ages in the past, and there may well be more in the future.

The situation is different if we can establish a connection between pollution and climate change. Thus it is argued that the increasing concentration of carbon dioxide and some other gases in the atmosphere is causing the earth to warm up due to what is called the greenhouse effect. The sun's rays enter the atmosphere and warm the earth and are trapped by carbon dioxide, which acts like the glass in a greenhouse. The warming of the earth then causes the climate to change and the sea levels to rise. The process is very complicated and can be calculated by computers using models of the mechanisms taking place in the atmosphere. The results suggest that the average world temperature will rise by about four degrees centigrade by 2100 and that the sea level will rise by about fifty centimeters. There is still much uncertainty about these figures, but they are the best predictions we have. Even if we discount them, there is the undoubted fact of increasing pollution created by fossil-fuel power stations, so we must consider the alternatives. This will be done in the next section.

## Renewable Energy Sources

All power stations burning coal, oil, or gas emit large amounts of carbon dioxide, which may be responsible for climate change, and a whole range of other poisonous substances. It is therefore important to see if there are alternative, nonpolluting energy sources.

Before doing this, we must remember that energy is precious and that billions of people do not have enough energy to support an acceptable lifestyle. If we find new energy sources, that still does not justify the continuation of our present energy-wasting lifestyles. We should all think about how we can reduce our energy consumption—by using less heat and air conditioning in our homes, by walking or cycling, and so on. While these measures by themselves cannot solve our energy problems, they can reduce their severity. Unfortunately most people take little notice of exhortations to save energy. Another method of reducing energy consumption is to increase the price of fuel, but this encounters fierce resistance and, if not carefully applied, could bear heavily on the poor.

There are several alternative energy sources, generally called renewable because they do not use up the resources of the earth and are quickly replenished. The most important is hydropower, which produces around 3% of the world's electricity. It depends on the presence of suitable rivers and has already been exploited to the practicable limit in developed countries. There are still many possible sites in developing countries, but even if all of them are put to use it is unlikely that the contribution of hydropower will much exceed the present fraction of energy supplies. Severely limited by geographical factors, tidal and geothermal energy generation contribute very little. Wave power has been extensively studied but has been found unpromising. Biomass, burning plants as fuel, is also a renewable resource; however, the process not only emits carbon dioxide but requires the use of valuable agricultural land. That leaves wind and solar power as the renewable energy sources with the greatest potential for increase. Despite great efforts over the last few decades, they still only contribute about 0.15% of the world's energy.

The amount of energy in the sunshine and rain, the wind and the waves is enormous. It is many thousands times more than our conceivable energy needs. The trouble is that it is very thinly spread, and to be useful to us it must be concentrated. In the case of hydropower, the valleys do the concentrating for us, and so it is a major energy source. In the other cases, we have to concentrate the energy ourselves, by building huge collectors, which are relatively expensive and dangerous. The windmills and solar panels have to be built in factories, and all manufacturing processes involve danger to some extent. The same applies to their construction and maintenance. Thus the term 'benign renewables' is misleading.

It takes many hundreds of windmills, spread out over many square miles, to equal the output of one coal power station. Inevitably windmills have to be sited in exposed positions, and they destroy the beauty of the countryside over much larger areas than power stations, which can be sensitively sited. The noise of the rotating blades is found to be unacceptable by people living near them.

The concept of renewable energy is very appealing to many people. It seems to be clean and efficient, safe and environmentally acceptable. Closer examination unfortunately reveals a very different picture. The renewables are simply incapable of supplying our energy needs and have many other disadvantages. There is, however, another energy source, and that will be considered in the next section.

## Nuclear Power

We have seen that coal, oil, and gas power stations burning fossil fuels emit many poisonous gases and also carbon dioxide, a possible source of climate change. The renewable energy sources, so attractive at first sight, turn out on closer examination to be incapable of supplying our energy needs. If that were all that could be said, the outlook would indeed be bleak. In 1939 scientists found that the nuclei of the element uranium, when bombarded with neutrons, can split into two pieces, with great release of energy. This is called fission. During the fission process, more neutrons are released, and these can cause further fissions, so that a chain reaction is established. This reaction can be controlled in a nuclear reactor so that the energy is released gradually and thereby generates electricity. Since this process was first demonstrated in the 1940s, nuclear power stations have been built in many countries and now generate about 20% of the world's electricity.

Like the other energy sources, nuclear energy can be assessed by considering its potential output, reliability, safety, cost, and effects on the environment. Nuclear power plants certainly have the capacity to generate the energy we need. Already 80% of France's electricity is nuclear, and around 50% in western Europe as a whole. These plants are very reliable and are among the safest of the ways to provide energy. They cost more to build than fossil-fuel power stations, but their running costs are less, and so their total costs are similar when averaged over their long working lives. Their costs would be even more favourable if the pollution due to fossil-fuel power stations were taken into account. They emit no noxious gases and so do not cause any pollution of the atmosphere.

The principal difference between nuclear reactors and other power sources is the presence of nuclear radiations. These radiations are all around us, in amounts that do us no harm. They are produced by some of the elements in our bodies, they come from the rocks, and they come from outer space in the form of cosmic rays. They are used in medical treatment and diagnosis and in many industrial processes. Extremely small amounts of nuclear radiation can easily be detected, and so the level of radiation can be controlled. Nuclear reactors do produce relatively small amounts of highly radioactive material, and techniques have been developed to ensure that it is safely disposed of underground where it can do no harm.

The design of nuclear power stations is constantly being improved. As natural uranium becomes scarce, fast-breeder reactors can be used that burn the plentiful uranium 238. A new design that is driven by a nuclear accelerator is being studied. This will be even easier to control and can burn up its nuclear waste, so that no radioactivity is produced. For the distant future, there are high hopes that fusion reactors will become practicable, and these will ensure almost unlimited supplies of energy.

When nuclear power stations were first built, they were hailed as the power source of the future. Since then a great change has taken place, attributable to several causes. First, the association with nuclear weapons has prejudiced many people against all things nuclear. A few notorious accidents, such as those at Three Mile Island and Chernobyl, have enhanced the fears, although modern reactors are designed differently and operate very safely. These fears have been magnified for political reasons, and now the governments in many countries are in a difficult situation. They know very well that they need nuclear power and that it is the only practicable way to reduce atmospheric pollution. Yet they also know that it will make them very unpopular if they permit the construction of more nuclear power stations. So they ignore the problem and hope that nothing drastic will happen before the next election. The responsibilities of governments and the churches in this extraordinary situation will be considered in the next section.

## The Responsibilities of Governments and Churches

It is the clear responsibility of governments to take action to ensure we will have future fuel supplies and also to see that this is done in a way that as far as possible does not pollute the earth. Most governments have now accepted the reality of climate change, and large conferences have been held in Rio and Kyoto to determine what should be done. As a result, governments have pledged to reduce carbon dioxide emissions: Britain, for example, plans to reduce emissions by 10% before 2010. However, it is not always clear how they intend to do this. Governments of course want to appear to be concerned about the earth, but there are strong commercial and political pressures against taking effective action. In addition, developing countries argue that since the developed countries didn't worry about pollution when they were developing their industries, why should they be prevented from acting in the same way?

Many governments, including that of the United Kingdom, periodically hold conferences that discuss energy conservation, fiscal measures, and the development of renewable sources, which, as we have seen, presently have limited ability to solve our problems. Amazingly, nuclear power, with its proven capacity to reduce carbon emissions, is never even mentioned. It seems to be a taboo subject. The reason for this is the known unpopularity of nuclear power; the government recognises that it will lose support if it even considers nuclear power.

This is of course a shameful situation, as it prevents effective action from being taken to tackle our energy problems. This provides a great opportunity for the churches, which should not be influenced by political considerations and can freely say what they believe to be true.

The churches have indeed issued many statements on nuclear power, but most of them are seriously inadequate. It is seldom realised that in dealing with scientific and technical questions it is essential to seek the advice of experts in all the relevant disciplines. Two notable exceptions are the statement 'Shaping Tomorrow' published by the Home Division of the Methodist Church[2] and the proceedings of a conference organized by the Pontifical Academy of Sciences. Both statements are based on extensive studies by very well-qualified experts, and both strongly endorse nuclear power, especially for the developing countries. Unfortunately they received very little publicity. The US bishops also issued a statement, but it was unsatisfactory in several respects.

In Britain, a conference entitled 'The Human Dimensions of Energy Problems' was organized by the Catholic Union and the Council for Justice and Peace, but the statement of the Pontifical Academy was not even mentioned. A prominent antinuclear lawyer was active in preventing the publication of many studies favouring nuclear power. With a few notable exceptions, such as *Month*, Catholic periodicals simply repeated the antinuclear line found in all the mass media. Thus a great opportunity of witnessing to the truth was thrown away.

If the Church is to be taken seriously, she must address the most important problems of our times, and these include the energy crisis and climate change. To do this, it is essential to use the many existing authoritative studies and to make use of the available expertise. Such studies should include detailed statistical data on the effectiveness of the various energy sources. This should enable the bishops to issue a statement calling on the government to rise above purely political considerations and to consider all aspects of the problem in an impartial way. The bishops could well emphasise the need to conserve energy and to take effective measures to protect the earth by reducing pollution to the lowest practicable levels.

Above all, the needs of the poor in the developing countries should be kept in the forefront. For them the presence of an adequate energy supply is not a luxury but a matter of life and death.

---

[2] *Shaping Tomorrow*, edited by Edgar Boyes (London: Home Mission Division of the Methodist Church, 1981).

## Reference

André Blanc-Lapierre, ed., *Semaine d'étude sur le thème Humanité et énergie: Besoins—ressources—espoirs.* 10–15 November 1980. Pontificiae Academiae Scientiarum scripta varia, no. 46 (Città del Vaticano: Pontificia Academia Scientiarum, 1981).

# CHAPTER 19

# Providing the Energy We Need and Caring for the Earth[*]

THE LECTURE by Mr John Gummer entitled 'Newman and the Environmental Imperative' published in *Newman* (May 2003) should convince readers that the problem of climate change must be taken seriously.[1] Serious discussion of this subject in the Church and in society as a whole is certainly long overdue.

The matter is so important that it should be taken beyond the level of rhetoric and generalities and an attempt made to face the hard questions. It is not good enough just to wring our hands and say we are heading for disaster. We need to make careful analyses and propose definite policies, and these are conspicuously lacking in Mr Gummer's article.

The central problem is to decide how we are to get the energy we need to sustain ourselves without at the same time polluting the earth and further changing the climate to an unacceptable degree. This requires a detailed analysis of all practicable energy sources in order to decide which can provide the energy we need cheaply, safely, and reliably without harming the environment. To make the necessary comparisons these analyses must be expressed in numbers wherever possible.

Many people are enthusiastic about what are called the renewable energy sources. Among these, wind power is recognised as the most

---

[*] Peter Hodgson, "Providing the Energy We Need and Caring for the Earth," *Newman* 51 (January 2004): 10.

[1] See the next chapter of this book starting on page 91.

promising. People imagine a peaceful rural landscape with some windmills whirling merrily away and supplying all the energy we need. That would be fine if were true, but if we are to make any progress, we must face reality: Wind can never provide the energy we need reliably and cheaply. At present, windmills provide less than 0.2% of Britain's energy, and even the optimistic target of this rising to 10% by 2010 still leaves the problem of how to get the remaining 90%. It is difficult to get an accurate estimate of costs, but it is very likely that wind power will cost at least two or three times what we pay now.

What about wave power? The energy in the sea is enormous, enough to supply our needs many times over, but the problem is how to harness it. A much-publicised device, costing over £1,000,000, is designed to produce 75 kilowatts. Oh wow! Fantastic! But if you know what numbers mean, that is enough to power twenty-five 3-kilowatt electric fires. In addition, it is very likely that the first storm will throw the whole contraption onto the beach as a pile of twisted metal.

Can solar power provide our needs? On a fine day, the sun provides an average of 200 watts per square metre, and this has to be collected and converted into electricity. It has been estimated that a collector the size of a large Jodrell bank radio telescope would be needed for each four houses.

In addition, these sources are unreliable due to changing weather conditions. It is sometimes said that the potentialities of the renewable energies will be increased by further research. It must, however, be recognised that whatever future improvements are made, they must be compatible with known facts and laws. Not even our present government can increase the intensity of solar energy on the earth's surface or make the sun shine for twenty-four hours a day.

It is a matter for regret that these are the facts, but they must be faced. As Feynman once remarked, 'If you don't like the world we live in, go somewhere else where the laws of nature are more to your liking'. But there is no other place.

So what shall we do? It is amazing that government-sponsored conferences on the problem of climate change consider a range of possibilities from higher taxes on energy to the whole range of renewables but do not even mention nuclear power. Whether we like it or not, it must be discussed, as it is the only practicable existing long-term option. Detailed studies show that it has the capacity to meet our needs. It produces energy reliably at a cost comparable to or less than oil and coal and has no adverse effects on the environment.[2] A recent study of the cost of energy from different sources, taking environmental effects into account, gave the following costs (in euros per kilowatt hour): 3.30 for nuclear, 4.24 for gas, and 4.81 for coal.[3]

After reviewing the detailed evidence supporting these statements, one may well ask why governments are not replacing the present polluting coal, oil, and gas power stations with nuclear power stations. Why is even the discussion of nuclear power stations taboo? The reason is very simple: The public has been so brainwashed by decades of left-wing-inspired propaganda against nuclear power that any political party that supported it would be unlikely to be successful at the next election.

So who is left to speak out and urge that this vitally important problem be considered fully and objectively? The people who know most about it, the people in the nuclear industry, are brushed aside with the remark: 'They would say that, wouldn't they?' This leaves the academic community and the churches.

At the end of the Second World War, nuclear scientists, particularly those who made the atomic bomb, were very conscious of the irreversible change that they had made to human society. On the one hand were the nuclear weapons and on the other the prospect of nuclear

---

[2] It is not practicable to summarise the detailed evidence here. There are two detailed studies by teams of experts that are essential reading for all interested in these problems:

(a) André Blanc-Lapierre, ed., *Semaine d'étude sur le thème Humanité et énergie: Besoins—ressouces—espoirs.* 10–15 November 1980. Pontificiae Academiae Scientiarum scripta varia, no. 46 (Città del Vaticano: Pontificia Academia Scientiarum, 1981). This important work has been summarised in P. E. Hodgson, 'Nuclear Power: Rome Speaks', *Clergy Review,* 68, no. 10 (February 1983): 49.

(b) The Methodist Church made a very professional study that was published as *Shaping Tomorrow,* edited by Edgar Boyes (London: Home Mission Division of the Methodist Church, 1981). A summary of the present position may be found in P. E. Hodgson, *Nuclear Power, Energy and the Environment* (London: Imperial College Press, 1999).

[3] *Nuclear Issues* 25 (25 March 2004): 3.

power. They considered that they had a moral duty to inform the public of these developments, and they organised associations devoted to this purpose. They arranged meetings; they wrote books and articles.

At first they were listened to, but by the 1970s they were overwhelmed by political propagandists. Now it is almost impossible for scientists to make themselves heard. In over fifty years of writing and lecturing on this subject, I have had only one serious debate on the prospects of nuclear power.[4] Usually when one writes an article or sends a letter to a newspaper, there is immediate response by activists who go on about nuclear wastes, Chernobyl, and radiation-induced leukaemia without apparently realising that these subjects have already been exhaustively discussed and evaluated at their true importance. These objections are given prominent publicity, and it rare for the scientists to be allowed to reply.

What about the Church? She certainly has the freedom and indeed the duty to speak out in defence of the truth, however unpalatable it may be to some people. Indeed the Vatican and the Methodist Church have spoken out in a highly responsible way, but what they said has been almost completely ignored. In 2003, I gave a lecture at the Gregorian University in Rome, and I asked those who had heard about the Vatican study of nuclear power to raise their hands. Not a single hand was raised. Why was that important document ignored by clergy worldwide and by the Catholic press? Unless the Church fearlessly grapples with such vital moral problems, she is easily seen as irrelevant by people everywhere, with the results we see all around us. It is just as serious to treat these problems as if they did not exist and to ignore what Rome has said so clearly and authoritatively.

God gave us the coal and oil and iron that made the Industrial Revolution possible. Now, when these energy sources are running out and we are becoming more conscious of the dangers of pollution and climate change, scientists and engineers have found the new energy source He has provided for us in the nucleus of the atom. Like all His gifts, they can be used for good and for evil, but we ignore them at our peril.

---

4 'Do We Need Nuclear Power?' debate between Dennis Anderson and Peter Hodgson, *Physics World* (June 2001): 16.

CHAPTER 20

# Climate Change*

THERE IS MUCH discussion at the present time about climate change. Impressive evidence has been presented that
indicates that the world's climate has changed dramatically
during the last few decades, with catastrophic results predicted
to occur during the present century. Conferences are held and articles
written on what should be done about this. There are wide differences
of opinion on the reality of climate change, and even more about the
action that should be taken. As usual, political and commercial considerations threaten to take precedence over the scientific and technological facts, and thus the likelihood of wise and effective action is reduced.

There is impressive evidence for the reality of climate change. Some
of this has been described in a recent article by Sir Ghillean Prance, former director of the Royal Botanic Gardens in Kew, London. He recalls
that in 1997 there were devastating floods in Mozambique and
Venezuela and quite serious ones in England. In other countries there
has been drought: In 1988 and 1989, the midwest of the United States
suffered drought-related losses estimated at $39 billion. In 1998, Hurri-
cane Mitch killed 10,000 people in Central America. More recently the
hurricane Katrina devastated New Orleans and its surroundings. The
average temperatures are rising in many countries: Of the five warmest
years ever recorded in the United Kingdom, four have been in the last

---

* Peter Hodgson, "Climate Change," *Fellowship of Catholic Scholars Quarterly*
(Winter 2001): 32.

89

decade. One result is that the growing season for many plants is increasing, with earlier development in spring, and autumn events being delayed. Birds and animals are also affected, and some species, unable to cope with the changes, have become extinct.

Such evidence raises many questions. Do these changes show that world climate is changing? If so, will it continue to change in the same way? Are these changes due to human actions? If so, what can we do about it?

By 'climate' we mean the sum of the many variables describing the condition of the atmosphere: the temperature and humidity of the air, the rainfall, the strength of the winds, and the clouds. These all change constantly, and we can take averages for a local region or for the whole earth. It is difficult to establish whether the average value of a fluctuating quantity is changing. It is possible to reduce the fluctuations by taking averages over space and time, but this also is not free from difficulties. It is possible, for example, for fluctuations of quite different time scales to be superimposed. Thus there may be small yearly fluctuations about a rising mean value superposed on large fluctuations with a timescale of centuries. This is indeed the case for temperature. The winters in England were apparently much colder a few centuries ago, when oxen were roasted on the frozen Thames. On a still larger time scale, we know that there has been a series of ice ages, when glaciers covered most of Europe. Even if we can establish that world temperatures are increasing, this does not imply that they will continue to increase; for all we know, they may have reached a maximum and will soon start to decline.

Climate is determined by many natural causes, but in addition, it may be affected by human actions. We cannot do anything about the natural causes, but if we can establish a causal link between human actions and climate change, we may have reason to expect the present changes to continue, and furthermore, we will have a strong incentive to take action to mitigate the harmful effects of climate change.

Such a causal link has been proposed. Extensive measurements have shown that the concentrations of carbon dioxide, methane, and some other gases in the atmosphere are steadily increasing: The annual increase of carbon dioxide is now 0.4%, that of methane 1.2%, that of nitrous oxide 0.3%, that of the chlorofluorocarbons 6%, and that of ozone about 0.25%. These are established facts. It is then suggested that these increases are responsible for global warming and that global warming is responsible for other climate changes and predicted effects, such as a worldwide rise in the sea level. The evidence for these suggestions needs careful consideration.

The connection between the increase in carbon dioxide and global warming is known as the greenhouse effect. The argument is that, as in a greenhouse, the sun's rays penetrate the atmosphere and warm the earth. Some of the heat emitted has a different wavelength that cannot escape because it is trapped by carbon dioxide, which is acting like the glass in a greenhouse. The trapped heat causes global warming.

While this argument is plausible, it needs careful scientific analysis before the conclusion can be established. Many scientists worldwide have been making detailed calculations using increasingly sophisticated models of the atmosphere. This is obviously a very complicated task. What, for example, do we mean by the 'temperature of the atmosphere'? We can measure the temperature at a particular place and height, but this needs to be done over the entire surface of the earth and for heights up to several miles. The best we can do is establish a grid of points and measure the temperatures at these points as a function of the time. Even a coarse grid contains millions of points, and the calculations are very time-consuming, even on the fastest computer. The more accurate we want our calculations to be, the longer they will take. In addition, the results may be very sensitive to the initial conditions; this is the 'butterfly effect'. The main uncertainty at present seems to be the effects of water vapour, which are greater than those of all the other gases combined. These are sensitively affected by changes in the cloud cover, which in turn changes the amount of solar energy absorbed or reflected.

The results of such calculations are published periodically by the Intergovernmental Panel on Climate Change, under the chairmanship of Sir John Houghton. With many qualifications, the conclusion of the latest work is that there is good evidence that the world's temperature is increasing, and it is predicted that the average temperature will rise by between 1.4 and 5.8 degrees centigrade by the year 2100.

One potentially devastating effect of a rise in world temperature is the consequent rise in sea level. It is predicted that sea level will rise by about 60 centimeters by 2100; if emissions can be controlled, this can be reduced to about 40 centimeters. Such increases in sea level will eliminate many islands, such as the Maldives in the Indian Ocean, and will inundate much of Bangladesh and some of Holland, just to mention a few examples.

The connection between the rise in temperature and the rise in sea level is not as simple as sometimes suggested. It has been attributed to the melting of the polar ice caps. However, the Arctic ice is floating; so when it melts it has almost no effect on the sea level, as Archimedes knew very well (although there are some very small effects due to differences in salinity between the ice and the sea). The Antarctic ice is partly on the continent itself and partly surrounding ice sheets. The interior of the continent is rather cold, typically from −40 to −60 degrees centigrade, so warming by a few degrees makes no difference. The surrounding ice sheets are somewhat warmer, but they are floating like the Arctic ice. The result is that the melting of the polar ice caps has little effect on sea level. Greenland has a more temperate climate, and its ice caps are now melting, causing a rise in sea level of 0.005 inches per year. However, if the ice caps slide into the sea, as indeed is happening, it causes the sea to level to rise.

Another possible effect is due to the expansion of the oceans when they are heated. It is seldom mentioned that land also expands when heated; whether this affects sea level depends on the relative expansion coefficients of the land and the sea. This is further complicated by the length of time it takes for warming to take place; this depends on the thermal conductivities of land and sea and by the presence of currents in the sea.

The result of all this is that the simple arguments concerning the connection between rise in world temperature and rise in sea level are inadequate, and so one has to rely on the complicated world climate models. It is not possible for those not actually making such calculations to assess the validity or the results and, one may add, not so easy even for those who are. There is additional uncertainty due to the possibility that changes in average world climate do not always take place smoothly. Thus it is possible that when some variable reaches a critical value, a large and irreversible change takes place, as when a kettle boils over or a house of cards collapses. While we cannot be absolutely sure what will happen to the climate in future, it has been suggested that there may be a sudden and catastrophic cooling of northern Europe due to a change in the flow of the Gulf Stream. Global warming could alter this flow by injecting more fresh water into the North Sea, and this could cause temperatures to fall by six to eight degrees centigrade. The North Sea would then be frozen for much of the year, and London would be like Siberia.

Such uncertainties are not uncommon in human affairs. Often we have to make decisions based on incomplete knowledge. It is easy to say that we must undertake more research and do nothing until we are sure we know what is the best thing to do. This is nearly always the worst decision. We must make our decision on the basis of the best knowledge we have, even if it is to some extent incomplete. Concerning climate change, the best knowledge we have is contained in the results of model calculations.

It is therefore prudent to consider what can be done to reduce emissions of what are now called greenhouse gases. These gases differ greatly in their concentrations and in their damaging effects per molecule. Thus chlorofluorocarbons are about 4,000 times more damaging than carbon dioxide. This has led to demands that they be banned as soon as possible. However, they are used in refrigerators, and so it is important that an effective substitute be found. The amount of carbon dioxide is so much greater that it accounts for more than 60% of the anthropogenic greenhouse effect, so efforts are concentrated on reducing carbon dioxide emissions. These come mainly from power stations burning fossil fuels, such as oil and coal, from wood burning, and from other industrial processes. Large international conferences, such as those held at Rio and Kyoto, encourage countries to reduce carbon dioxide emissions. Many countries have already pledged that they will reduce emissions by a stated amount in a given time.

Such decisions are highly political. Of course countries want to appear in a good light and to be seen to care for the earth, but they are not so keen to take actions that will be commercially unfavourable. Reducing emissions can be very costly and can reduce the competitiveness of an industry. Developing countries understandably protest that the developed countries achieved their industrial power without worrying about polluting the earth, and now they want to impose strict controls that will gravely hamper the growth of the developing countries. Politicians have committed their countries to reduce pollution but are reluctant to take the politically unpopular decisions necessary to achieve this.

The only ways to reduce carbon dioxide emissions are to reduce energy demand and to replace fossil-fuel power stations with nonpolluting energy sources. Energy demand can be reduced by exhorting people to conserve energy, to walk or ride their bicycles, to switch off lights when not needed, to use less heating and air conditioning, to use energy-efficient machines, and so on. All this is highly desirable for many reasons, and the potential energy savings from such activities are enormous, but human nature is such that exhortation is ineffective unless there is some clear and preferably short-term gain. An incentive to save energy can be provided by increased taxes, but experience shows that these have to be rather severe, and hence highly unpopular politically, if they are to have an appreciable effect. Governments are therefore very reluctant to try to enforce energy savings in this way. The recent revolt in several European countries against fuel price increases indicates the strength of the emotions that can be aroused.

It is therefore essential to eliminate fossil-fuel power stations and to replace them with nonpolluting energy sources. Particular attention is devoted to the renewable sources, as these do not exhaust the resources of the earth and are generally nonpolluting. Foremost among these is hydropower, which provided 3% of world energy in the year 2000. Unfortunately this requires suitable rivers, and most of these have already been used wherever practicable, especially in the developed countries. It is thus unlikely that the contribution of hydropower can be appreciably increased. Tidal power and geothermal power are similarly severely limited by geographical considerations. The potential of wave power has been studied and has proved unpromising. This leaves wind and solar power as the favoured renewable sources. The amount of energy in the wind and in solar radiation is enormous, but unfortunately it is thinly spread and requires large collectors to concentrate it to a usable form. The result is that the present contribution of wind and solar power to world energy is 0.15%. Nevertheless they do have valuable small-scale applications, and these should be developed wherever practicable.

If that was all that could be said, the prospects of satisfying world energy needs without polluting the earth and causing drastic climate change would be dim indeed. However, there is another source to be considered, namely, nuclear power. This source provides about 20% of world electricity, is very reliable, and, almost completely nonpolluting. The countries that have built nuclear power stations have dramatically reduced their carbon dioxide emissions. Thus France is about 80% nuclear and has halved its carbon dioxide emissions; Japan (32% nuclear) has achieved a reduction of 20%, while the United States (20% nuclear) has reduced them by 6%. The emission of sulphur dioxide is also drastically reduced by replacing coal power stations with nuclear. The British government has set a target of a 10% cut in carbon emissions in the period from 1990 to 2010. By 1995, a cut of about 6% had been achieved; this was due to the increase in nuclear output by 39% from 1990 to 1994. In the next few years, however, emissions are set to rise as the older nuclear power stations reach the end of their lives, and no new ones are being built. There is thus no hope that the targets will be met, and the situation is similar for the United States.

In view of these facts, it is remarkable that conferences that are held to discuss how to combat climate change discuss fiscal measures, and wind and solar power, but make no mention whatsoever of nuclear power. The only explanation is that governments are aware that nuclear power is politically so unpopular that they would lose support if they advocated the construction of new nuclear power stations. It is thus important to ask why nuclear power stations are so unpopular. One reason is the association with nuclear weapons, and another is fear of radioactivity, particularly in the form of nuclear waste. It is certainly true that nuclear reactors produce relatively small amounts of highly radioactive material, but ways have been developed to deal with it so that it will never come into contact with humans and cause harm. These psychological problems should be resolutely faced and not simply ignored as if they do not exist. Reality can be avoided for some time, certainly during the period before the next election, but in the end, the problems will have to be faced and the longer this is postponed the more difficult it will be to solve them, if indeed it is not already too late.

# CHAPTER 21

# The Energy Crisis
# and Nuclear Power*

THE SCIENTIFIC and technological advances of the present century have brought about an unprecedented increase in the standard of living of millions of the world's inhabitants. This has, however, created new problems that have recently come into prominence. We are acutely aware that the resources of the earth are finite, that we are using them up at an accelerating rate, and that many of our activities are polluting the earth to an unacceptable degree. If we persist on our present course, we are heading for an irreversible disaster that will make our present worries pale into insignificance.

These problems are widely debated; books, articles, and television programmes tell us about the threats to our fragile earth. Many organisations demand rapid action. It is recognised that the Church has a vital part to play in this debate and indeed has already made important contributions. In many respects, however, she has failed to rise to the occasion and does no more than repeat the errors and distortions of the media.

A basic requirement, generally not well understood, is that those who contribute to these debates should have a certain level of understanding of the basic scientific and technological facts. Without this it is impossible to say anything useful, and it is very easy to talk dangerous nonsense. It is thus necessary to begin by briefly summarising the

---

* Peter Hodgson, "The Energy Crisis and Nuclear Power," *Blackfriars* 73, (1992), 121.

present situation and, with this as a basis, move on to wider political and moral questions. It is convenient to begin with the energy crisis, a definite and clear-cut problem that faces us now. We all depend on energy in its various forms, and the amount available to us is directly related to our standard of living. Hundreds of millions of people are now living in the direst poverty because they do not have enough energy. Where are we going to get the energy to give them life and to support us all in the next century?

The Gulf War brought home to us once again the dangers of relying too heavily on oil. There is increased understanding of the pollution hazards associated both with oil and with coal-burning power stations. Should we think again about nuclear power, or does it also have unacceptable hazards?

The problems of energy and the environment are by no means new. In ancient times the forests of the Mediterranean lands were cut down for fuel. Many parts of North Africa once supported large populations and are now desert. Later, the forests of central and northern Europe were also cut down for fuel.

During the Middle Ages and the following centuries, coal was increasingly mined and replaced wood as the major source of energy. Coal mines, with associated deposits of iron ore, made possible the Industrial Revolution. In the present century, oil has replaced coal as the major source of energy, but it is expected that world oil production will reach a maximum in a very few decades.

World population is increasing rapidly. The rate varies greatly from one country to another, but overall it is doubling every thirty or forty years. Energy consumption is rising even more rapidly due to improved living standards. Thus our energy needs are increasing while our oil production is beginning its decline. Where will our energy come from in the next century? This is an exceedingly urgent problem that faces each country in one form or another.

There are two ways to tackle this problem, and both are needed. One is to stop the demand for energy from rising so rapidly; the other is to increase energy production. Our standard of living is closely related to the energy supply. We need energy to cook our food and heat our homes as well as to make possible our transport, industry, and communications. At present the richer nations of the world, mainly in Europe and North America, are using ten to twenty times as much energy per capita as people in the poorer countries of Asia, Africa, and South America. If this unbalance is to be redressed, world energy supply must be greatly increased.

We waste an enormous amount of valuable energy, and so much of it could be saved by conservation, restraint, and increased efficiency. It is not easy to see how this can be brought about on a sufficiently large scale. Energy demand can be reduced by rationing or by increasing prices, but this would affect the poorer people. Some form of differential tariffs would be worth considering.

Energy conservation is essential, but it is not sufficient on its own. Conservation alone cannot solve our energy problems, though it can make them more soluble. Even with the most efficient use of energy, we still need vastly more than we produce at present. Where is it to come from?

It is possible here only to sketch the more important considerations governing our choice of energy sources. We need all the energy we can get, subject to the above criteria, and so it is necessary to exploit all sources to the limit. There is no single solution, and the optimum mix of energy sources varies from one country to another.

Our list of energy sources includes wood; coal; oil and its associated gas; hydroelectricity; and nuclear, wind, solar, wave, tidal, and geothermal power. Some of these are relatively minor sources, very useful in some places for specialised purposes. But here we must concentrate on major sources of power, those capable of providing energy for large cities and manufacturing industries.

We cannot expect to solve our problems with wood or oil because they have passed or will soon pass their maximum capacity. Hydroelectric power is very important, especially in mountainous countries like Norway and Switzerland, but due to the fact that it requires suitable rivers, it can never provide more than about 3% of the world's energy. Tidal power is similarly limited by the rather small number of suitable river estuaries. Geothermal energy is even more limited, as hot springs are found in few countries. Wave power is still in an early experimental stage, but it does not look very promising.

Wind and solar power need careful consideration. Windmills have been used for a very long time and can provide power to grind corn or to generate electricity. Solar power is most efficient when it is used as a source of direct heat, as in the roof panels that heat domestic water. It is possible, but much less promising, to use it to generate electricity. Unfortunately wind and solar power are not reliable.

We are therefore left with coal and nuclear power as our possible major energy sources of the future. At present it is not a matter of choosing between them because both will be needed for the next few decades. It is nevertheless useful to compare them closely because the decision that faces each country is whether the next new power stations are to be coal or nuclear.

Coal is a familiar source of energy, and there are enormous deposits in many countries. Certainly coal has the capacity to provide large amounts of energy for several hundred years.

The cost of coal power has been compared with that of nuclear power by detailed studies in many countries, and the figures vary between the two being about equal to coal being about twice as costly as nuclear. This comparison is on the basis of the costs of mining the coal or uranium, constructing the power plant, and delivering electricity to the consumer, with the same financial assumptions about inflation and rate of return on capital.

However, this comparison does not give the whole picture unless environmental considerations are also included. Coal power stations emit large quantities of poisonous gases that contribute to acid rain, and this affects all living things, from plants to people. They also produce carbon dioxide, which contributes to the greenhouse effect. A recent study evaluated the costs of the pollution caused by coal power stations; it concluded that if these costs were included in the calculations, the cost of coal power would be quadrupled. There has been much discussion about the imposition of a tax on coal power to allow for this. If this were done realistically, it would very greatly increase the price of coal power. Even then the damage to the environment would remain, unless the tax encouraged the use of an alternative source of power.

Safety is a most important consideration. Unfortunately no source of power is completely safe; all involve risks to both the workers and the public. These risks can be expressed by evaluating the number of people killed or injured in the course of generating a specified amount of electricity. These include casualties due to mining, transport, and construction. One such study showed that the numbers of people killed in the course of generating 1,000 megawatt years of electricity is about 40 for coal, 10 for oil, 1 for nuclear, 3 for hydroelectricity, and 5 for solar and wind power. For man-days lost due to injury, the figures are 1,000 for coal, 400 for oil, 8 for nuclear, 40 for hydroelectricity, and 70 for wind and solar power.[1] These figures are subject to many uncertainties, but they serve as useful guides. Coal is dangerous because of the hazards of mining. Oil is dangerous because of rig explosions. Hydroelectric power is dangerous because of the possibility of dam bursts. Wind and solar power, misleadingly called the 'benign renewables', are unexpectedly dangerous because of the very large number of units that have to be built to give the same output as a coal power station, and all manufacturing processes involve hazards.

Coal power stations thus compare rather poorly with nuclear power stations from the point of view of safety, and the pollution they cause has already been mentioned. Nuclear power stations, on the other hand, have minimal effects on the environment.

These considerations led many countries, especially those—such as France—that have no oil or suitable coal reserves of their own, to embark on large programmes of nuclear power station construction. In many countries most of the electricity is now obtained from nuclear power. In France this figure is about 80%, and in many other countries it is around 40%. Nuclear power has replaced coal as the major source of electricity in western Europe. Worldwide, there are over 400 nuclear power reactors in 25 countries, with a total generating capacity of 324 GWe (gigawatts-electric). By far the largest nuclear power programme

---

[1] Herbert Inhaber, 'Risk of Energy Production' (Ottawa: Atomic Energy Control Board, 1981), 169.

is in the United States, although it produces only about 16% of their electricity. In the UK, the figure is about 20%. The total number of operating years is now over 10,000 worldwide.[2]

In spite of this, there is widespread opposition to nuclear power. After Chernobyl, some countries, such as Sweden and Switzerland, resolved to build no more nuclear power stations and to close existing ones as soon as possible. Subsequently these countries found that the alternatives are even more unacceptable, and so the policy is being quietly reversed.

The reasons for the opposition to nuclear power are of many different types. The power locked in the atomic nucleus first made itself known by the bombs on Hiroshima and Nagasaki, and the fear that a nuclear reactor could run out of control and blow up like a bomb is not far below the surface. Fortunately this is physically impossible, but Chernobyl showed that a hardly less catastrophic failure can occur.

Nuclear reactors are sometimes seen as symbols of all that is evil in technological society: They are viewed as huge, menacing, and inhuman. We prefer things to be small, friendly, and beautiful. We are familiar with the dangers of coal and oil, and they seem infinitely preferable to the unknown dangers of nuclear power. Better the devil we know.

The special characteristic that provokes most unease is nuclear radiation, which we cannot see or feel until it has done the damage. The same applies to electricity, and we are used to that; perhaps some day we shall get used to nuclear radiations.

It is not only nuclear power stations that produce nuclear radiations. They are all around us all the time. The cosmic rays that enter the earth's atmosphere from outer space, and the rays emitted from radioactive rocks and from chemicals in our own bodies are all nuclear. We irradiate ourselves when we have a chest X-ray, when we have radium therapy, or when a radioactive tracer is used in diagnosis. They all do us no detectable harm and provide a standard for us to judge the hazards of radiations from a nuclear reactor.

---

[2] Power Reactor Information: International Atomic Energy Agency, Vienna; *Nuclear Issues* 23, no. 5 (May 2001).

In a nuclear power station uranium undergoes fission and produces heat, leaving behind what are called 'fission fragments'. After a time, these accumulate and slow down the reactor, and so they have to be removed. To do this, the spent fuel rods are taken out and processed to separate out the fission fragments from the remaining uranium. They constitute nuclear waste and are useless and highly radioactive.

The method of dealing with nuclear waste so that it is rendered harmless is now well understood. First it is stored above ground until most of the radioactivity has decayed, and then it is fused into an insoluble glassy substance, encased in stainless steel cylinders, and buried underground in a dry stable geological formation. There is then no danger that the radioactivity will escape and return to the surface. After many thousands of years, the level of radioactivity will decay to the same level as the surrounding rocks.

Another category of nuclear waste comes from industry and medical procedures that involve radioactive materials. This has a low level of radioactivity, and it can be put into drums and safely buried on land or in the sea.

There is widespread and justified concern at the reports of increased numbers of cases of leukaemia around nuclear installations such as Sellafield. It is known that intense nuclear radiation can cause serious injury because it destroys cells in the body. However, the increased level of radiation around Sellafield is a very small fraction of the natural background radiation, so it is difficult to understand how it could be responsible. The natural background varies from one place to another, depending on the type of soil. In Cornwall, for example, it is about twice the national average, and yet the incidence of leukaemia there is below the average.

If nuclear radiation is not the cause of the leukaemia, then what is? It should first be remarked that many surveys in other countries have found no significant evidence of increased incidence of leukaemia around nuclear sites. Furthermore, clusters of leukaemia cases are found in other parts of the country where there are no nuclear installations. This suggests that there is some other cause. One possibility is that the leukaemia is due to a viral infection that occurs when there is a large movement of population, as occurs when a large factory is built in a relatively remote area. Comparative studies of similar population movements not associated with nuclear power also show increased leukaemia frequencies, which supports this hypothesis. Another possible cause is chemical effluents from nearby industries.

The nuclear reactors now in operation are thermal reactors in which slow neutrons cause fission in uranium 235, an isotope constituting only 0.7% of natural uranium. Uranium is quite widespread in the earth, usually in rather poor ores, and could become increasingly costly to mine in a few decades as the richer ores are used up. It will then become economic to change to fast reactors that are able to use the remaining 99.3% of natural uranium. This will effectively increase the supplies of fissile material by a factor of about sixty. The energy stored in spent fuel rods in Britain alone is equivalent to that in the North Sea oil. Prototype fast reactors are already in operation, and the technology is well understood, so it is likely that they will begin to take over nuclear power production in about thirty or forty years.

Ultimately, the hope for the world's energy supply is that fusion reactors will prove possible. The basic physics is that nuclear particles called deuterons and tritons can fuse together, releasing a large quantity of energy in the process. These particles will fuse, provided the temperature is high enough; the problem is to hold them together for long enough. Many experiments are in progress to see if this can be done using high magnetic fields, for example, as is being done in the JET (Joint European Torus) Laboratory at Culham near Oxford. Very encouraging progress has been made, and it is hoped that the next generation of machines will pass the break-even point, where more energy is produced than is used to run the machine. Since deuterons are found in ordinary water, and tritons can be made in the reactor, the energy available from fusion reactors is virtually limitless.

It is sometimes said that one of the great advantages of fusion reactors is that they produce no radioactivity. This is unfortunately untrue. There are of course no fission fragments, but the fast neutrons emitted from the reactor, which carry most of the heat produced, will inevitably induce radioactivity in the surrounding material. Some of my own research is devoted to finding ways to minimise this induced radioactivity. Recent studies show that it is likely that the radioactivity due to fusion reactors will be substantially less than that associated with fission reactors.

After the problems of making fusion reactors have been solved, it will be a long time before fusion power becomes a reality. Preliminary studies are already in progress, but it will be several decades before the first fusion power station is built. Hopefully they will be contributing substantially to world energy needs in the latter half of the present century.

Thus it seems that nuclear power in its three main forms—thermal, fast, and fusion—is well able to supply the foreseeable world energy needs. Whether it will is not just a matter of physics, technology, and economics, but also of politics, and this will now be considered.

It might well be considered providential that nuclear power was developed just in time to take over from oil as the main source of the world's energy. Coal, the only major alternative, is increasingly recognised to be seriously polluting, and the other energy sources, though important in various ways, are unable to produce energy in the quantities required.

Yet, instead of thanking God for this new source of energy and devoting all our efforts to making it generally available, especially to the poorer countries of the world, we find widespread apprehension and determined opposition.

Initially, in the 1950s, nuclear power was welcomed with enthusiasm. Scientists lectured and wrote articles explaining the new source of energy and were assured of a hearing. The engineers mastered the technology of nuclear power and set to work to build nuclear power stations. In a few decades nuclear power was producing more than half the electricity of western Europe, and there were large nuclear power programmes in many countries, especially in the United States.

Why, then, such determined opposition? As already mentioned, some of the reasons are association with the bomb, the unfamiliarity of nuclear radiations, and the reports of leukaemia cases near nuclear installations. Another reason is the sensationalism of the mass media. It is so much more interesting to read about radioactive horrors than the boring and unintelligible explanations of the scientists.

The accident at Three Mile Island and the disaster of Chernobyl certainly loom large in the public mind, giving rise to the fear that at any moment a nuclear reactor may run out of control, with deadly consequences. The Chernobyl disaster was partly due to a bad design and partly to operator incompetence and flagrant disregard of the operating instructions. The reactor was designed to produce plutonium for weapons as well as power and was built in a hurry. In certain operating regions it was thermally unstable, a feature that would never be accepted in the West. The political climate prevented the Soviet Union from making full use of international expertise in reactor design, and the pressure to build rapidly prevented internal protests.

On the evening of the accident, the operators wanted to make an experiment at low power, in the unstable region. They were afraid that the reactor might automatically cut out and spoil their experiment, so they switched off the safety devices. To make their experiment, they removed more control rods than permitted, and disaster followed. The design of the reactor should never have allowed such actions. It was a disaster that should never have happened, and it is attributable more to politics than to technology.

Politics is indeed one of the strongest forces behind the opposition to nuclear power. A coal strike brought down the government of Mr Heath, but the subsequent attempt to bring down the government of Mrs Thatcher failed, largely because of the nuclear power stations. If you want to maintain the political power of the coal miners, then you must hate nuclear power.

There is also an international dimension to the opposition to nuclear power. Western Europe is heavily dependent on imported oil; it could be brought to its knees by an interrupted oil supply. Nuclear power could gravely hinder this strategy, so it must also be attacked. Recent political developments have indeed undercut most of this strategy, but its effects remain.

These are some of the motivations behind the relentless media campaign against nuclear power, the continual scares about nuclear radiations, the spectre of nuclear accidents, and the hysteria about nuclear waste. What is needed is simply a careful assessment, in each country, of its energy needs and the best ways of satisfying them, taking into account the capacity, cost, safety, reliability, and effects on the environment of all possible power sources.

It is tragic that the campaign against nuclear power gravely hinders this process. We are all the losers. If the correct decisions are not taken, energy is more costly, pollution is increased, the environment is destroyed, and lives are needlessly lost. As always the chief sufferers are the poor of the world. As the price of oil rises, they can no longer afford it and have to spend much of their time gathering fuel to cook their food. Valuable organic matter is burnt instead of being returned to the land; the soil is impoverished and becomes desert.

In Britain, our national priorities are distorted by what is called the 'nuclear debate'. Large sums are spent on marginally improving the safety of Sellafield, whereas the same amount of money spent, for example, on improving motorways could save many more lives. There is strong opposition to the burial or sea disposal of low-level nuclear wastes but no proportionate concern about the pollution caused by coal power stations and other industries. It is ironic that coal power stations emit more radioactivity than do nuclear power stations, but that is never mentioned. Scientists who advocate more-balanced policies cannot get a hearing. Environmentalists have yet to realise that of all power sources, nuclear has the least damaging effect on the environment.

These arguments about relatively minor hazards of nuclear power distract attention from the really important problems concerned with how we are to obtain enough energy to maintain our standard of living and, even more important, how we can help poorer countries. How are they to get their energy without nuclear power? How can it be paid for, and how can the design and operation of those power stations be controlled so as to ensure safe operation without infringing their sovereignty?

The churches could play an important role by encouraging objective studies that take full account of the scientific data. This was done by the Pontifical Academy of Sciences when it convened a meeting of experts at the Vatican in 1980 to study world energy needs and resources. The conclusions of this study were presented by the Holy

See to the International Atomic Energy conference in Vienna in 1982. In his speech, the head of the delegation, Mgr Peressin, emphasised the urgency of the problem and recommended that 'all possible efforts should be made to extend to all countries, especially to the developing ones, the benefits contained in the peaceful uses of nuclear energy.'[3] A further meeting on energy for survival was held in 1984. The proceedings of these conferences, a mine of accurate information, were soon published but remain virtually unknown and have received no publicity or discussion.

Largely due to the influence of a prominent antinuclear campaigner, eminent in a nonscientific discipline, the Catholic press in Britain (with the honourable exception of the *Month* under the wise editorship of Mr Hugh Kay) failed to encourage informed discussion of the energy crises and nuclear power in the light of Christian principles. Instead, it has done little more than repeat the errors of the mass media, nearly always refusing a hearing to scientists who tried to correct them. The churches thus missed a great opportunity to contribute to the welfare of society, which they could have done simply by providing a forum for the truth.

An immense amount of damage has already been done. Eventually, as the effects of pollution become more evident, when our industrial competitors outstrip us with the help of cheap nuclear power, when poorer countries plunge further into famine because we have selfishly used up their oil and neglected to help them directly, then we will see clearly the effects of the antinuclear campaign. It is possible to ignore the realities of life for a while, but eventually there is an awakening, and the slower it is, the greater the cost. Our children and grandchildren, if they survive, will suffer the consequences of our folly.

---

[3] Statement of the Holy See to the International Conference on Nuclear Power, Vienna, 13–17 September 1982. International Atomic Energy Agency, Paper CN-42/449.

CHAPTER 22

# Flickers of Sanity*

## The Belmont Abbey Conference

A CONFERENCE was held at Belmont Abbey in February 2004 on the theme 'Faith and the Environmental Imperative', responding to the document 'The Call of Creation' issued by the bishops of England and Wales.[1] At the conference, four papers were given by very well-qualified speakers, and the texts and discussions have been published by the Newman Association.[2] The speakers at the conference emphasised the familiar and laudable concerns to care for the earth, but in addition there was a clear recognition of the need to take seriously the possibility of using nuclear power to provide the energy we need. This makes the Belmont meeting particularly notable, and it is this aspect that will be emphasised here.

The conference was opened by the abbot of Belmont. Describing himself as just a simple monk, he went to the heart of the problems facing the world today by describing the purchase of a Peruvian mango at a local supermarket for £1.50. As it happened, he had worked in Peru for many years, and from the sticker on the mango, he knew that it

---

* Peter Hodgson, "Flickers of Sanity," *St. Austin Review* (November/December 2004): 33.
[1] Copies available from Colloquium (CaTEW) Ltd., Publications Department, 39 Eccleston Square, London, SW1V 1BX. An analysis of this document was published in the *St Austin Review* (November 2002).
[2] This report is available from Mr Robert Williams, 77 Bearcroft, Weobley, Hereford HR4 8TD, price £6.50. An audiotape recording is also available.

came from a factory near his Peruvian monastery, a factory that has not been paid for the mangoes for three years. God gave the earth to man, and that is how the poor are treated. This story was a salutary reminder that the needs of the poor should lie at the centre of all our discussions about the energy crisis, the greenhouse effect, and climate change.

The second paper, devoted to global warming and climate change, was given by Sir John Houghton. As chairman of the International Commission on Climate Change, no one is more qualified that he to speak on this subject. Furthermore, he set his remarks in a Christian context. He began by summarising the evidence for climate change and global warming due to the greenhouse effect and stressed the necessity to reduce emissions of carbon dioxide and other greenhouse gases. These gases are largely due to the so-called fossil fuels—coal, natural gas, and oil—so it is necessary to replace these fuels with clean energy sources. As alternatives, he suggests 'the generation of energy from renewable energy sources and the development of means to prevent carbon dioxide from conventional generation from entering the atmosphere'. Let me say at once that I would be delighted if all our energy needs could be met by windmills and solar panels, but, alas, that is sheer fantasy. It is part of the vocation of a Christian to face reality, however unpleasant it may be.

Sir John gave several examples of possible renewable energy sources, such as biomass—'fast-growing willow plantations cut down and used in power stations. Or forest residues or waste materials can be used'. Another possibility is the use of underwater tidal turbines. Such sources must, however, be shown to be cost-effective; Sir John gives no figures, and existing studies of such methods are not encouraging. He also advocates solar cells, saying that 'a one-metre-square photovoltaic solar array can be used by a household or a village in the third world to provide the necessities of life without any connection to a main power supply at all'. This sounds fine; would that it were true. The sun provides on average about 200 watts per square metre, and this can hardly provide the necessities of life for a village.

In his lecture, Sir John does not mention nuclear power, but in the panel discussion, he points out that 'nuclear energy does not produce any significant greenhouse gases or carbon dioxide, which is good' and adds that 'I think that it is a great pity that we can't have a proper debate about nuclear energy'. Regrettably he does not follow this up and initiate the debate. Instead, he lists what he calls the three problems of nuclear energy: 'First of all, there is a danger of accidents; secondly, there is the danger of nuclear material—and nuclear waste material—and what you do with it; and thirdly there is the problem of proliferation of nuclear material of a bomb-making kind into the hands of terrorists'. The following comments may be made:

1. There is no method of energy generation that is free of danger, so it is necessary to compare these risks. Studies have shown that of all sources, nuclear is the second safest, gas being the safest.[3]

2. The methods for the safe disposal of nuclear waste are well understood and pose no particular technical difficulty.

3. The issue regarding bomb-making is indeed a serious problem, but the cat is out of the bag, and a moratorium on nuclear power will not solve it. It would, in fact, make it much worse, as it will exacerbate the political tensions arising from the scramble for the remaining oil.

These and other objections to nuclear power could well have been discussed further at the meeting. As Sir John remarks, the danger posed by the large stocks of military-grade plutonium could be removed 'by burning it in nuclear power stations. So that would be a good thing to do in my view, and it would provide quite a lot of energy in the meantime while we get renewable energy online'.

In the third paper, Bishop John Oliver began by supporting Sir John's emphasis on the needs to reduce carbon dioxide emissions and went on to declare, with a most welcome recognition of reality that

> I am personally absolutely convinced that we have to have another generation of nuclear power stations. I just don't think that we are

---

[3] Herbert Inhaber, 'Risk of Energy Production' (Ottawa: Atomic Energy Board, 1984). A 1995 study by the Scherrer Institute in Switzerland of serious accidents put nuclear power first in terms of safety, with gas second.

going to get anywhere near the 60% [reduction in $CO_2$/greenhouse emissions] if we've got to phase out 22% of our present clean generating capacity and at the same time still cut down our existing fossil-fuel [usage, which generate] pollution. I just don't think it is achievable'. He reminded us, 'We are desperately dependent on the natural gas coming increasingly—as the North Sea dries up—from governments which I wouldn't like to bet tuppence on, frankly. Whatever you do is risky. The worst risk is climate change; the second worst risk, I think, is the interruption of our supplies of natural gas. The risk associated with nuclear [power], I think, is less than those; that is my personal opinion'. He went on: 'I am sorry, personally, that the government White Paper did not say we have to go straightforwardly for the new generation of nuclear power; I think we have to.

This paper was much more than a flicker of sanity; it was a blaze of realism.

The remainder of Bishop Oliver's paper was devoted to a general survey of God's plan for creation and our responsibilities toward it.

The fourth paper, by Mrs Ellen Teague, 'Responding to the Cry of Creation', provided an extended account of our duties toward the environment and the practical actions that can be taken. By means of several examples, she showed what personal action can achieve.

All the papers provided most welcome food for thought about one of the most pressing problems of our times.

A contributor to the panel discussion was Richard Davies, who said that he believed that 'all nuclear power stations will have ceased to be generating in the UK by 2020'. He added that he did not support nuclear energy because 'it is very expensive' and said that 'there are many cost-effective things that give benefit to many people that we can do, such as energy efficiency and community renewable energy'. This assertion about the cost of nuclear power is not borne out by several recent studies. For example, a commission was appointed by the Belgian government to examine the costs of energy generation in various ways. They took into account the cost of fuel, investments, operation and maintenance expenses, atmospheric air pollution, noise, and greenhouse gases, and the results were, in pence per kilowatt-hour: 2.34 for coal,

1.74 for gas, 2.39 for wind power (off-shore), 2.36 for wind power (on-shore), and 1.25 for nuclear power. Many other studies gave broadly similar results. Energy efficiency is of course desirable, but energy still has to be generated. The cheapest renewables produce energy at about twice the cost of nuclear power.

The contribution of the churches to the nuclear debate provides little cause for satisfaction. A magnificent lead was given by the Pontifical Academy of Sciences, which arranged a meeting in November 1980 that brought together many of the world's highest authorities to study the theme of humanity and energy.[4] The papers presented, the discussions, and the conclusions were published in a massive volume of 770 pages. This authoritative and detailed survey of a vital and urgent problem could have formed the basis for an informed and valuable contribution by the Church to the nuclear debate. Although it emphasised that 'we have no time to waste', this pioneer study was almost entirely ignored. At a recent lecture at the Gregorian University in Rome I asked the members of the large audience to raise their hands if they had heard of this work. Not a single hand was raised. It was almost entirely ignored in this country, apart from an article in the *Clergy Review*.[5] The conclusions of the Pontifical meeting were given additional authority when they were made the basis of the contribution of the Holy See to the International Conference on Nuclear Power held in Vienna on 13–17 September 1982. The leader of the Vatican delegation, Mgr Peressin, stressed that the economic growth of third world countries seems 'to be impossible without some applications of nuclear energy', and therefore 'my delegation believe that all possible efforts should be made to extend to all countries, especially the developing ones, the benefits contained in the peaceful uses of nuclear energy'.[6] In spite of this, no

---

[4] André Blanc-Lapierre, ed., *Semaine d'étude sur le thème Humanité et énergie: Besoins—ressources—espoirs*. 10–15 November 1980. Pontificiae Academiae Scientiarum scripta varia, no. 46 (Città del Vaticano: Pontificia Academia Scientiarum, 1981).

[5] 'Nuclear Power: Rome Speaks', *Clergy Review* 78 (February 1983): 49.

[6] Statement of the Holy See to the International Conference on Nuclear Power, Vienna, 13–17 September 1982. International Atomic Energy Agency paper CN-42/449.

mention was made of the work of the Pontifical Academy at a conference entitled 'The Christian Dimensions of Energy Problems' organised by the Catholic Union and the Commission for International Justice and Peace and held in England in April 1982.[7]

Instead of following the lead of Rome, the Catholic press, with very few exceptions,[8] has simply repeated the antinuclear propaganda spread by the Soviet Union with the object of weakening the Western world.

The churches are thus losing a great opportunity to make a vital contribution to the general well-being and especially to the needs of the poor. The government knows very well that nuclear power is unpopular and is terrified of losing the last shreds of its dwindling support by any actions favouring nuclear power.[9] The bishops are free to speak the truth without fear, and if they are persecuted for it, then it is a special sign of Christ's favour. In this case they can perform their duty simply by following Rome's lead.

Sir John rightly deplored the antagonism between the pronuclear and the antinuclear people, but pointed the way to a solution by advocating the construction of more nuclear power stations 'before we get renewable energy online'. Only nuclear power can provide the energy the world desperately needs without intolerable pollution and climate changes, so, with the needs of the poor in mind, let us get on with it as an interim measure. Meanwhile, let the supporters of the renewables work hard to develop them to the point when they will be demonstrably safer, cheaper, more reliable, and kinder to the environment than nuclear power. Then we can phase out the nuclear power stations and enjoy the benefits of the renewables. Everyone should be

---

[7] *The Christian Dimensions of Energy Problems,* papers delivered at a conference held in Brunel University, Uxbridge, London, April 1982 (Commission for International Justice and Peace, 1983), 82.

[8] Notably the *Month,* when edited by Mr Hugh Kay.

[9] The Conservative Party is not much better. When he was minister for the environment, Mr John Gummer hindered the development of nuclear power by forbidding exploratory drillings to investigate the suitability of a proposed site for the disposal of nuclear waste. Now he gives lectures on caring for the earth (see chapter 19). A summary of one lecture was published in the *Newman* (May 2002), and a commentary was published in the same journal in January 2004.

happy with this scenario, the only difference between the two groups being that one believes that this happy state will come soon and the other that it will probably never come. However, if we accept this suggestion, we should then no longer be bothered by controversy and can get to work on our chosen route.

The Belmont meeting hopefully constitutes a watershed, as it provides the beginning of a sane response to the urgent problems facing the world. There is still much to be done. A flicker of sanity is better than the darkness of the previous night.

## Suggestions for Further Reading

Peter Hodgson. *Nuclear Power, Energy and the Environment.* London: Imperial College Press, 1999.

John Houghton. *Global Warming: The Complete Briefing.* Oxford: Lion Publishing, 1994.

# CHAPTER 23

# Nuclear Radiations
# at Nagasaki*

AN INTERNATIONAL CONFERENCE on nuclear radiations and their effects, organised by the Radiation Education Forum, was held in Nagasaki on 22–26 August 2004. It brought together many nuclear scientists, leaders of the Japanese nuclear industry, and high school teachers from many countries. The principal theme was the need for education in the potentialities of nuclear radiations both in schools and in society as a whole.

The opening session was devoted to two talks: one entitled 'School Education and the Energy Problem' by Professor Akito Arima (formerly professor of physics at Tokyo University and subsequently president of Tokyo University, director of Riken Laboratory, Senator and Minister of Education, and now director of the Japan Science Foundation), and one entitled 'Nagasaki and Radiation: The Atomic Bomb and Chernobyl' by Professor Shigenobu Nagataki (Nagasaki University).

I was privileged to give the first invited lecture, on the topic 'Energy, the Environment and Nuclear Power', showing the growing need for energy if our living standards are to be maintained and the poorer countries provided with the energy they so desperately need. All energy sources must be considered and evaluated according to their capacity, reliability, cost, safety, and effects on the environment. At

---

* Further discussion may be found in *Proceedings of the Third International Symposium on Radiation Education,* Nagasaki, 22–27 August 2004. Kashiwa: Japan Atomic Energy Research Institute.

present we rely mainly on the fossil fuels of coal, oil, and natural gas, but they all contribute to the greenhouse effect that is responsible for climate change, and they all poison the earth. Hydropower is limited by the availability of suitable rivers, and the so-called renewables, such as wind, solar, tidal, and wave power are unreliable, costly, and environmentally objectionable and contribute only a few percent of our energy needs. This lecture, together with that of Professor Arima, showed that only nuclear power can provide the energy we need, and this forces us to consider the effects of nuclear radiations.

Nuclear radiations are widely feared principally because of the atomic bomb and because of accidents that have occurred at nuclear power stations. It should be emphasised that nuclear radiations are perfectly natural phenomena; we are constantly irradiated by the cosmic rays and by radioactivity in the earth and in our own bodies. In spite of this, there is a widespread belief that all radiation is harmful, that even small doses can cause cancer, and that genetic effects can threaten future generations. On all these questions new data were provided at the conference.

The consequences of this radiophobia are very serious. At the conference, Professor Klaus Becker (vice-president of Radiation Science and Health) cited the lack of acceptance of nuclear power, quasi-terrorist actions against transport of nuclear materials, purely politically motivated blocking of an almost completed high-level waste repository at Gorleben, and the premature phasing-out of some of the world's safest and most reliable nuclear power plants.

The evidence concerning genetic effects came from Professor Sohei Kondo (Osaka University), who had visited Nagasaki soon after the bombing and saw the devastation. He has studied the effects of the bombing for forty years and has accumulated a vast amount of information concerning the survivors and their descendants. He presented data on 20,000 children of atomic bomb survivors exposed to an average dose of 400 millisieverts. The numbers of the genetic indicators—chromosome abnormalities, mutations in blood proteins, childhood leukaemia, congenital defects, stillbirths, and childhood deaths—showed no difference between the children of the atomic bomb survivors and a control group. There is thus no evidence of genetic effects of nuclear radiations.

There has been much controversy about the effects of small doses of radiation, which cannot be measured directly. The effects of large doses can be measured, and it is the usual practice to assume a linear relationship between dose and damage and thus estimate the effects of small doses. In practice no one worries about such small doses, but the linear-dose hypothesis has several important consequences. Thus if it is used to calculate the effects of radiations due to Chernobyl, one can multiply the very small probability of causing damage per person by the population of Europe and so obtain the estimates of tens of thousands of cancer cases that have been widely publicised.

A new technique for evaluating the effects of small radiation doses by observations of the mechanism of damage to individual cells was described by Professor Ludwig E. Feinendegen (Henrich-Heine University). The new data show conclusively that the linear-dose assumption hypothesis is incorrect; at low doses there is an additional quadratic term. Furthermore, there is impressive evidence that small doses of radiation are actually beneficial, because they activate the natural immune system. This effect has indeed been noticed for many years but has been discounted because it seems counterintuitive. For example, people living in areas of high background radiation show no evidence of detrimental effects; thus in Kerala the life expectancy is seventy-four years compared with 54 years for India as a whole. Aircrews are exposed to higher doses of the cosmic radiation, and their union asked for compensation. Studies of the mortality rates of 19,184 pilots in the period 1960–1996 showed, however, that the mortality rates actually decreased with dose. Such results show that the mass deportations after the accident at Chernobyl, which caused so much suffering, were largely unnecessary.

A direct result of the linear-dose hypothesis is the setting of unreasonably strict limits on radiation exposure in many industries, thus greatly increasing their costs, leading in turn to reluctance to accept vital radiodiagnostic and radiotherapeutic irradiations and restricting the use of radiation in industry and research.

It is important that these new results should become widely known, and many lecturers at the conference described the educational programmes in their own countries. The general experience is that the more people know about nuclear radiations and their effects, the more supportive of nuclear power they become.

In the final session it was stressed by several speakers that it is important to understand the origin of the present antinuclear campaigns. It is sometimes maintained that the origin of the opposition to nuclear power is the fear of atomic bombs. This is not so. In the immediate postwar years many nuclear scientists devoted considerable efforts to educate the public; they wrote articles and books and organised lectures and exhibitions. They founded the Federation of Atomic Scientists in the United States and the Atomic Scientists' Association in Britain. I participated in this work as a member of the Council of the Atomic Scientists' Association from 1952 to 1959 and edited the *Atomic Scientists' Journal* from 1953 to 1955. The result of these efforts was general public enthusiasm for the potentialities of nuclear power, and people looked forward to the atomic age.

This all changed as a result of a well-planned and large-scale campaign by the Soviet Union designed to weaken the West. It was clear to the Soviet leaders that the economy of the West depended on sufficient supplies of energy, so they first tried to jeopardise the supplies of oil by destabilising the Middle East. It then became apparent that the West could obtain much of its needed energy by developing nuclear power, and so this became a prime target. A massive propaganda campaign was therefore launched against nuclear power. The dangers of nuclear radiations were vastly exaggerated, the disposal of nuclear waste was declared to be an unsolved problem, and so on. The campaign was cleverly designed to enlist the support of well-meaning people who lacked the technical knowledge to understand the way they were being deceived. It was spearheaded by Communist parties throughout Europe and taken up by left-wing parties everywhere. Finance on a massive scale to support the campaign was provided by the Soviet Union.

While attacking the Western nuclear power programme, the Soviet Union feverishly built its own nuclear reactors, designed to produce weapons-grade plutonium as well as power. Their reactors were so poorly designed, so hurriedly built, and so poorly operated that the disaster of Chernobyl was almost inevitable.

As a result of this campaign the public mood swung round from support of nuclear power to the opposition that still exists today and continues to weaken the West in numerous ways. The new results presented at this conference expose more clearly the falsity of the propaganda that brought this about.

# CHAPTER 24

# Perfectly Safe?

OF COURSE we want everything to be perfectly safe: Anything that is not perfectly safe should be banned! Unfortunately life is not as simple as that; almost nothing is perfectly safe. We all know this very well in our everyday lives. We often have small accidents, and sometimes serious ones. We know that it is not perfectly safe to cross the road or even to walk along the pavement. We know that road accidents are tragically frequent. These accidents are more or less under our control in the sense that they are often our own fault, and we have come to terms with them.

Obviously we must do all we can to reduce accidents to the minimum, but then we accept that some hazards remain.

What is much more serious is that in some other areas we seem to have lost all sense of proportion and become paranoid about relatively small dangers while remaining complacent about much larger ones. A prime example was the recent scare about the safety of consuming beef and lamb. Quite properly, the government consulted scientists about the risk of contracting disease from infected meat. In the circumstances, no scientist is going to say that it is perfectly safe, because there is a small chance of infection, and he would be disgraced if someone did indeed succumb. So the scientists report to the government that there is a small danger. The minister of health then makes a speech saying that he is not going to approve the sale of any meat that carries any risk of infection, and he bans the sale of such meat. Naturally the farmers are furious, and people can find no meat in the shops. There is a deadly logic in this process, which if carried to extremes could lead to almost everything being banned.

In such circumstances, the minister should have the courage to repeat the conclusions of the scientists, saying that there is some small danger, and let the people make up their own minds whether to take the risk or not. In addition, it is of course essential to see that the source of the infection is removed, and this may require legislation if the industry does not do it itself.

It is the same with nuclear radiations. People have become so paranoid about the word 'nuclear' that hospitals have renamed the diagnostic technique that used to be called 'nuclear magnetic resonance'. There is a great fear of nuclear radiations but almost no attempt to understand them. We have all been exposed to nuclear radiations all our lives. Some radiations come from radioactive materials inside our bodies, some from radioactive rocks and soil, some from the cosmic radiation, and some from medical treatment. This is the background radiation that no one has ever worried about. Background radiation varies by factors of ten or more from one place to another. In Cornwall it is about twice as high as in the rest of the country, but this does not stop people from going there for their holidays. The intensity of cosmic radiation increases with altitude, so the higher you go the more you receive. Mountaineers seldom bother about this, and neither do people travelling by air. All these doses are so small that the deleterious effects, if any, are minuscule.

The situation changes dramatically when people hear that a nuclear waste disposal site may be built near their home. Immediately they are up in arms, and it is useless for authorities to say that the amount of radioactivity will be so small and buried so deep that it cannot harm anyone. Protest groups are formed, and the member of parliament for the area is worried. He tells the prime minister that if this proposal goes ahead, he will probably lose his seat in the next election. So the minister decides to cancel the proposal. The situation is now so out of hand that even a proposal to make a trial boring to see if the proposed site is suitable for safe waste disposal is rejected.

Similar fears surround nuclear power stations, although the amount of radioactivity they emit is minuscule, even less than the amount of radioactivity emitted by coal power stations. Why are there no similar protests when a coal power station is built? Such is the fear of nuclear radiations that Sellafield has been forced to spend hundreds of millions of pounds to save one hypothetical statistical life, while a few thousand pounds spent on motorway crash barriers are known to save one actual statistical life. It is called a hypothetical life because it depends on the hypothesis that the hazard is proportional to the dose, so that there is some hazard even for extremely small doses. This is by no means proved, and there is even some evidence to the contrary. In this way, the pressure of public opinion is actually killing people.

In these and many similar cases the sensible course of action depends on the assessment of probabilities, and this does not come naturally to most people. Nevertheless it is vitally important to assess hazards numerically, even if the numbers are only approximate. This is far better than having no numbers at all.

Some time ago there was a study in which people were asked to rank twenty possible hazards in order of importance. The results were compared with a similar ranking by experts, and these were quite different. What most people thought were serious risks are rather small ones, and conversely.

It is important to take care about what we eat and to avoid polluting the environment, but our guides must be objective analyses, not feeling and emotion.

# CHAPTER 25

# The Shadow of Chernobyl

THE FIFTEENTH anniversary of the accident at Chernobyl has provided the opportunity for more articles, and one of these featured prominently in a colour supplement. It portrays in graphic detail the continuing suffering of those living in the region around Chernobyl and still forbidden to return to their homes. Many are in poor health and are afflicted by leukaemia and other maladies that they ascribe to nuclear radiations.

Like most articles on the subject, it is rather lacking in numerical data that would enable the reader to assess the seriousness of the tragedy. Thus it is frequently said that the radiation levels are so many times normal, without defining what is meant by 'normal' and in particular whether this increased level is itself dangerous. The radiation in Cornwall is more than twice the normal level in the UK, yet no one suggests evacuating Cornwall.

The level of the natural background radiation varies by factors of 10 or more from one place to another, depending on the type of soil and the height above sea level. Thus the average dose in the UK from the background radiation is 2 millisieverts per year, in Spain it is about 5, and in Finland it is about 8. This is so low that it causes no detectable harm. Many chemicals are essential and beneficial in small doses but harmful in large doses, and there is some evidence that the same is true for nuclear radiations. The permitted occupational level established by the International Committee for Radiation Protection is 20 millisieverts per year. A recent study of the population of Kerala, India, an area with a natural level of 200, showed cancer rates lower than in the country as a whole, together with increased life span.

The health of people living in the Chernobyl region has been exhaustively studied by international medical authorities under the auspices of the United Nations, and they found no evidence of adverse health effects attributable to the disaster apart from increased incidence of leukaemia, which is easily curable. The deaths, mentioned in the article, among the liquidators (those who worked to clean up the area) are about the number expected from natural causes.

So why are all these people still suffering so severely? There are several reasons. First, they were suddenly uprooted from their homes and have not been allowed to return. They are afraid to eat certain foods, and so their health suffers. Everyone ill is treated as a 'victim of Chernobyl' and so claims compensation, although of course most illnesses have nothing whatever to do with the Chernobyl disaster. Everyone in the region thus has a vested interest in attributing all their troubles to the disaster, and this is encouraged by the authorities for political reasons. Journalists of course thrive on sensational scare stories, and most people are repelled by objective medical and numerical studies.

It is thus increasingly clear that most of the suffering is attributable to psychological causes due to misinformation and inept handling of the situation. Of course the authorities had to tackle an extremely difficult situation with inadequate knowledge, so they do not deserve to be blamed severely. There is less excuse for ignorance now.

None of this should be taken as minimising what was undoubtedly a terrible disaster, but just as politics was responsible for it in the first place, so politics and general incompetence has greatly increased the suffering of the people in the region. The more misleading information is published, the worse for the people concerned.

In addition, continual repetition of exaggerated scare stories strengthens the opposition to nuclear power, which objective studies show is the only practicable way to ensure our future energy supplies and thus to maintain our standard of living, without the damage to the environment that is the inevitable consequence of all alternative practicable sources of energy.

## CHAPTER 26

# Facts and Fantasies

I WAS RECENTLY asked to review the draft of a science booklet addressed to children of twelve to fourteen years. The author was an experienced science teacher. The text therefore gives an insight into the ideas current among those responsible for the education of the coming generation.

Most of the text is well done, but the section on energy problems are particularly revealing. Sections are devoted to the acid rain, pollution, and global warming due to the burning of the fossil fuels (coal, oil, and natural gas), and the importance of reducing these hazards is stressed. Among the 'valuable conservation measures' to reduce greenhouse gas emission is 'the use of alternative energy sources, such as windmills and wave machines', but no figures are given for the reductions attributable to either source. Such figures would show a very small reduction for windmills and no reduction for wave machines. The effects of switching to nuclear power stations is not even mentioned, although there are detailed statistics available for the massive reductions in greenhouse gas emissions due to this policy. For example, France, which generates 80% of its electricity from nuclear power stations, has reduced its greenhouse gas emissions by 50%. Other countries with fewer nuclear power stations have reduced their greenhouse emissions by correspondingly smaller amounts.

Concerning the renewable energy sources, we read in the introductory paragraph that 'in the sunnier regions solar power is becoming more and more important, and in the windy western parts of Britain, wind power makes a large contribution to our energy requirements'. A few pages further, we learn from a table that the percentage contribution from solar heating is 0.35% and from wind 2.7%, figures that are neither important nor large. Nuclear power is not mentioned in the introductory paragraph, and in the table its contribution is given as 12%. No region or date is given for the figures in the table, but recent figures for the UK are around 25%.

The importance of conserving fuel reserves is emphasised, and one way to do this is by using 'alternative, renewable energy sources', with no mention of nuclear power. There is a useful table that gives figures for the use of coal, gas, and oil in the UK from 1970 to 2000, but again no mention of nuclear power. There is a section on the poisonous properties of sulphur dioxide, a gas emitted from fossil-fuel power stations, but no mention of the large reductions in sulphur dioxide emission that occur when fossil-fuel power stations are replaced by nuclear power stations.

In the leading paragraph of the section entitled 'What Is Science?' there is a list of what we learn from science, including 'why the government is thinking of building more windmills'. The implied answer is 'To provide the energy we need'. Scientific studies show, however, that this source is able to provide only a small fraction of our needs at a high cost. The reason is not scientific at all. The government must be seen to do something; it cannot promote nuclear power because it is politically unpopular, and so it advocates wind power instead.

Taken together, these extracts uncritically accept and repeat many of the fantasies about energy that are current today. They give enthusiastic support to wind and solar power, and show such a strong distaste for nuclear power that it is never seriously considered. There is a marked preference for qualitative rather than quantitative statements. There are few numbers, and some of those given tend to contradict the author's general statements. If this account of the energy crisis had been allowed to stand, it would have passed the fantasy world to the next generation, putting the government under more pressure to adopt policies that will ultimately lead to ruin.

Most of us would be very happy if we could get all our energy needs from windmills and solar power, but the facts show otherwise.

We all have to live in the real world, and it is hard and not always to our liking. Education should teach the next generation to face reality and not feed the young with fantasies.

# CHAPTER 27

# Have I Been Wasting My Time?*

### Reflections on the Nuclear Debate

MODERN SCIENCE is affecting us in numerous ways. Our lives are very different from those of people living just a few decades ago. The pace of change presents us with many have problems, and we to make decisions that require some knowledge of what is involved.

Scientists are very aware of this, and most of us consider that we have a duty to share our knowledge with society as a whole, so that wise decisions can be made. This responsibility was felt acutely by those who had taken part in the development of nuclear weapons during the war, and they made strenuous efforts to inform the public by lectures, books, and articles. In addition to the dangers of nuclear weapons, there was also the promise of nuclear power stations to generate unlimited energy for peaceful purposes.

As a graduate student in the late 1940s, I joined the Atomic Scientists' Association, which was dedicated to this purpose. In those days the public was very receptive, and articles by enthusiastic journalists looked forward to the coming atomic age.

---

* Peter Hodgson, "Have I Been Wasting My Time?," *St. Austin Review* (June/July 2004): 37.

Some years later, the public view of nuclear power began to change as a result of a sustained propaganda campaign,[1] magnified by several nuclear reactor accidents, from the relatively minor one at Three Mile Island to the very serious one at Chernobyl.[2,3]

Newspapers and TV programmes were, and still are, filled with inaccurate and misleading stories about nuclear power. The emphasis is on shock and horror, with no attempt to provide balanced factual information, which most readers find either unintelligible or boring. Scientists often try to correct these stories, but it is like sweeping leaves against the wind. The corrections are seldom published, and when they are, there is usually another letter criticising the correction, and the subsequent reply of the scientist is not published. I have had this experience many times. It would be easy to conclude that it is all a waste of time, since the media are more interested in sensation than in truth.

Many churches realised that nuclear power raised several vital moral problems, and the churches made statements on the desirability of this new source.[4] Most of the statements were based on inadequate knowledge of the scientific and technological facts and so, with two exceptions, were worse than useless. It was not realised that a detailed familiarity with the facts, which can be obtained only by years of serious study, is essential if a useful statement is to be written. This should give pause to any church leader, however eminent, who makes a statement on a scientific matter without ensuring that he is adequately briefed. If the experts are ignored, they can either remain

---

[1] The motivation for this campaign is to weaken the West. Like all well-planned campaigns, it is based on truths taken out of proportion. This ensures that it is supported by well-meaning people who do not realise they are being misled.

[2] See my *Nuclear Power, Energy and the Environment* (London: Imperial College Press, 1999), 82–94.

[3] To date I have written three books and over 100 articles on nuclear power. Many have been reprinted in *The Roots of Science and Its Fruits* (London: Saint Austin Press, 2003). See especially 'Green Energy—Facts and Fantasies' (111), which lists and answers many of the objections that are so frequently made.

[4] Many of these statements are given, with commentary, in my review 'The Churches and Nuclear Power', August 1984 (unpublished).

silent, thus failing to carry out their responsibilities, or publish critical analyses, which they can do with devastating accuracy.

The two exceptions were the study in 1980 arranged by the Pontifical Academy of Sciences[5] and the study published by the Methodist Church in Britain,[6] both of which were based on detailed studies by many scientists and technologists. The papal study was used as the basis of the submission of the Holy See to the international conference held in Vienna in 1982 on nuclear power.[7]

One might have expected that the documents giving the results of these studies would be widely welcomed and publicised. So far as I know, they were totally ignored in Britain, and the press, including the Catholic press, went on repeating the current propaganda against nuclear power. I urged a leading Catholic weekly to publish a summary of the results of the papal study, but this suggestion was rejected. So far as I know, the only summary published was an article that I wrote for the *Clergy Review*.[8] In April 1982, a conference entitled 'The Christian Dimensions of Energy Problems' organised by the Catholic Union and the Commission for International Justice and Peace was held in Brunel University, Uxbridge, UK.[9] This was a magnificent opportunity to publicise and discuss the papal document. Astonishingly, it was not even mentioned, although at my suggestion an extract from the conclusions was included as an appendix to the proceedings of the meeting.

The 'nuclear debate', as it is euphemistically called, continues today, but in spite of numerous books and articles, it is notable that there are

---

[5] André Blanc-Lapierre, ed., *Semaine d'étude sur le thème Humanité et énergie: Besoins—ressources—espoirs.* 10–15 November 1980. Pontificiae Academiae Scientiarum scripta varia, no. 46 (Città del Vaticano: Pontificia Academia Scientiarum, 1981).

[6] Edgar Boyes, ed. *Shaping Tomorrow* (London: Home Mission Division of the Methodist Church, 1981).

[7] Statement of the Holy See to the International Conference on Nuclear Power. Vienna, 13–17 September 1982. International Atomic Energy Agency Paper CN-42/449.

[8] 'Nuclear Power: Rome Speaks', *Clergy Review* 78 (February 1983): 49.

[9] The Christian Dimensions of Energy Problems, proceedings of the conference organised by the Catholic Union and the Commission for Justice and Peace, April 1982.

still people without any scientific training who think that they know more about scientific and technical subjects than those who have spent years studying them, and they do not hesitate to air their views in public. Scientists exposed to this often feel like the Russian physicist Lev Landau when he saw such writings. He replied to one of them:

> Your remarks consist of naivetes that are of no interest whatever. Modern physics is a tremendous science, based primarily on a large number of experimental facts. You are patently almost completely unacquainted with this science, and you attempt to explain physics phenomena, about which you know little, with meaningless phrases.
>
> Modern physics is a complicated and difficult science, and in order to accomplish anything in it, it is necessary to know very much. Knowledge is all the more needed to advance new ideas. What you call new ideas is simply the prattle of an ill-educated person. If you are seriously interested in physics, first take time to study this science. After some time you yourself will see how ridiculous are the sentences that come out of your typewriter.
>
> The arguments advanced by you are unfortunately absurd in the highest degree. It would even be difficult to explain where the errors lie in your letter. For God's sake, before you start expounding on the universe, acquire at least the most elementary ability to read a physics text; all you do now is to put yourself in a ridiculous situation.[10]

Similar remarks were made by the Catholic physicist Pierre Duhem when he attended a conference on philosophy and science:

> My opinion was asked concerning the scientific part of the problem. Then, I squarely told all those good Catholic philosophers that if they obstinately continued talking of science without knowing of it a single word, the freethinkers would hold them up to ridicule; that in order to speak of questions where science and Catholic philosophy touch one another, one must have done ten or fifteen years

---

[10] I. M. Khalatnikov, ed., *Landau: The Physicist and the Man* (New York: Pergamon Press, 1989), 283.

study of the pure sciences, and that, if they had not become men with deep scientific knowledge, they must remain silent.[11]

The theoretical physicist Wolfgang Pauli was not one to mince words. When he was asked for his opinion of a certain paper, he replied with terse brutality, 'It is not even wrong'.[12]

Such remarks reflect the astonishment and anger of scientists who encounter people who hold forth on subjects they do not understand and do not even try to understand. By years of study and careful observation, scientists have learned a few things about the natural world. In this ecumenical era, when every belief is held to be equally valid and deserving of respect, scientists appear to be arrogant when we affirm that certain beliefs are true. It is, however, not arrogance but humility to accept it as it is. We do not claim infallibility and we are all prone to make mistakes, but as soon as we recognise them, we correct them and learn from them. There is always in the scientific community a careful scrutiny of all claims to new knowledge and an extensive web of cross-checking that ensures errors will be corrected as soon as possible.

There is another characteristic of science that stands in stark contrast to other areas of discourse. Science is progressive. Each generation of scientists builds on what is already known and always reaches out into the unknown. To become a successful and respected scientist, it is necessary to become familiar with what is already known. More colloquially, you must know the score. If you show ignorance of what has already been achieved, your papers will be rejected by journals, you will receive no research grants, and you will not be accepted as a member of the community of researchers.

This is in sharp contrast to what is called the 'nuclear debate', where the same old arguments are brought out again and again, without any sign that they have already been discussed and refuted a thousand times. People with no scientific knowledge pick up a few ideas from the mass media and immediately use them to pour scorn on scientists who are trying to write objective accounts. If we do not understand or if we

---

[11] S. L. Jaki, *Uneasy Genius: The Life and Work of Pierre Duhem* (Dordrecht: Martinus Nijhoff, 1984), 114.

[12] W. H. Cropper, *Great Physicists* (Oxford: Oxford University Press, 2001), 257.

want to know about something, the proper action is to ask someone who does know for an explanation, and scientists would be glad to do their best to provide one. This would make possible a useful debate. In over fifty years this has never happened to me; instead, one receives a barrage of critical remarks from people who obviously know nothing about the subject. The only useful debate I have had was with Professor Anderson on whether we need nuclear power.[13]

Is it too much to expect that the people concerned about nuclear power take the trouble to learn about it before publicly criticising scientists who are doing what they can to tell them about the potentialities and hazards of the ways it can be used to generate a reliable energy source?

[13] Peter Hodgson and Dennis Anderson, 'Do We Need Nuclear Power?' *Physics World* (June 2001): 6.

# CHAPTER 28

# The Church and Nuclear Power

## Introduction

THE ACHIEVEMENT of a nuclear chain reaction by Fermi in 1942 made it possible to harness the power of the atomic nucleus for the good of mankind. In the immediate postwar years the potentialities of nuclear power were enthusiastically welcomed, as described in the second section of this book, 'History', and people even spoke of the dawning of the nuclear age. Subsequently, as described in the third section, 'Nuclear Physics', this dream vanished and was replaced by widespread opposition to nuclear reactors. Many Christian churches recognised that the energy question is of great importance for the future of mankind, and they organised conferences to study the problems and to make recommendations.

## The Postwar Acceptance of Nuclear Power

In the immediate postwar years the scientists who had been engaged in the atomic bomb project realised that the release of the power of the atom held great potentialities for good and for evil. As the bomb project was highly secret, the general public knew nothing about these possibilities, and so the scientists realised that they had a great responsibility, indeed a moral duty, to do all that they could to inform the public. They lectured, wrote articles, and organised exhibitions for this purpose and founded the Federation of the Atomic Scientists in the United States and the Atomic Scientists' Association in Britain.[1]

Nuclear power soon became accepted as a pollution-free and relatively cheap source of electricity, and many countries began to build nuclear reactors. Within a few decades about 400 nuclear power reactors worldwide were producing about 20% of the world's electricity. The fraction generated in this way varied greatly from country to country, depending on the availability of alternative sources such as coal, oil, and natural gas and on the technological sophistication of the country.[2]

## The Campaign against Nuclear Power

Within a short time the popularity of nuclear power suffered a dramatic reverse. The Soviet Union, then one of the world's two superpowers, was engaged in an intense struggle to capture the allegiance of western Europe and, through the activities of the Communist Party, especially in France and Italy, very nearly succeeded in doing so. Part of their strategy was to weaken the West economically by disrupting their oil supplies, and to this end they worked to destabilise the Middle East, where much of the oil originates. They then realised that the burgeoning growth of nuclear power threatened this strategy by providing an alternative source of energy. They therefore embarked on a sustained campaign to discredit nuclear power.

This campaign was orchestrated with great skill and subtlety. Their arguments against nuclear power were based on true statements that were grossly exaggerated and on other statements that were conceivably true but almost impossible to falsify. They were greatly helped by the fact that true and false statements in this area can be separated only by

---

[1] I am not unfamiliar with this work because I was a member of the Council of the Atomic Scientists' Association from 1952 to 1959 and edited the *Atomic Scientists' Journal* from 1953 to 1955.

[2] There are numerous books on nuclear power, and references to some of them may be found in my books *Nuclear Physics in Peace and War* (London: Burns and Oates, 1961), *Our Nuclear Future?* (Belfast: Christian Journals, 1983), and *Nuclear Power, Energy and the Environment* (London: Imperial College Press, 1999). The scientific and technological data supporting the statements in this article may be found in these books.

measurements that give results expressed numerically, and people generally find these considerations boring or unintelligible, whereas the scare stories used in the campaign are exciting and readily understood.

An example of the first type of statement concerns the dangers of nuclear radiation. There is no doubt that high doses of nuclear radiation are dangerous and can be lethal, but this is not the case for small doses. Indeed, we are all continually subjected to small doses of radiation from radioactivity in the earth, from the cosmic radiation, and from radioactivity inside our own bodies. These radiations cause us no perceptible harm and so provide a standard dose for comparison with other sources. Thus, whenever the dangers of nuclear radiation are discussed, it is essential to quote the measured dose in order that a proper comparison can be made.

Another example is provided by the disposal of nuclear waste, which is often billed as the most serious unsolved problem. It is indeed true that the used fuel rods that are periodically removed from nuclear reactors are highly radioactive, but the methods used to handle them are well known and present no insuperable technical difficulties.

Especially after the accident at Three Mile Island, and still more after the disaster of Chernobyl, nuclear reactors are considered to be highly dangerous. The former accident was attributable to a design fault that has been rectified, and the latter was also due to poor design and operator error. Western reactors are now so designed that such disasters cannot occur.

An example of the second type of story, namely those based on statements that are conceivably true but almost impossible to disprove, is provided by the consequence of the assumption of proportionality between radiation dose and death rate. Using this assumption, it is easy to show that tens of thousands of cancer deaths are attributable to disasters like Chernobyl, and many such stories have been published.[3] The proportionality assumption, though apparently reasonable, has always been implausible, if only because the body can easily cope with

---

[3] This has been shown by Professor Feinendegen in work presented at the Third Symposium on Radiation Education held in Nagasaki on 22–27 August 2004.

small injuries but not with massive ones. Quite recently, however, the proportionality assumption has been shown to be false.

When this campaign against nuclear power was first launched, scientists were amazed, but what happened has been described by Professor Bernard Cohen, a distinguished nuclear physicist:

> First let us consider the cast of characters in the battle. One of the main interests in life for a typical anti-nuclear activist is political battling, while the vast majority of nuclear scientists have no inclination or interest in political battling, and even if they did they have little native ability or educational preparation for it.... While the former was making political contacts and developing know-how in securing media cooperation the latter was absorbed in laboratory or field problems with no thought of politics or media involvement. At this juncture the former went out looking for a new battle to fight and decided to attack the latter; it was like a lion attacking a lamb.
>
> Nuclear scientists had long agonised over such questions as what safety measures were needed in power plants, and what health impacts their radioactivity releases might cause. All the arguments were published for anyone to see. It took little effort for the anti-nuclear activists to collect, organise selectively, and distort this information into ammunition for their battle. Anyone experienced in debate and in political battles is well prepared to do that. When they charged into battle wildly firing their ammunition, the nuclear scientists first laughed at the naïveté of the charges, but they didn't laugh for long. They could easily explain the invalidity of the attacks by scientific and technical arguments, but no one would listen to them. The phoney charges of the attackers dressed up with their considerable skills in presentation sounded much better to the media and others with no scientific knowledge or experience. When people wanted to hear from the scientists, the attackers supplied their own—there are always a few available to present any point of view, and who was to know that they represented only a very small minority of the scientific community. The anti-nuclear activists never let it be made clear who they were and who they were attacking. The battle was not billed as a bunch of scientifically illiterate political activists attacking the community of nuclear scientists, which is the true situation. It was rather represented as 'environmentalists'—what

a good, sweet, and pure connotation that name carries—attacking big business interests (the nuclear industry) which were trying to make money at the expense of the public's health and safety.

The rout was rapid and complete. In fact the nuclear scientists were never even allowed on the battlefield. The battlefield here was the media, which alone have the power to influence public opinion. The media establishment swallowed the attackers' story hook, line, and sinker, becoming their allies. They freely and continually gave exposure to the anti-nuclear activists but never gave the nuclear scientists a chance. With constant exposure to this one-sided propaganda, the public was slowly but surely won over. The public was driven insane with fear of radiation; it became convinced of the utterly and demonstrably false notion that nuclear power was more likely to kill them than such well-known killers as motor vehicle accidents, cigarette smoking, and alcohol; that burying nuclear waste, actually a very simple operation, was one of the world's great unsolved problems; that, contrary to all informed sources, the Three Mile Island accident was a close call to disaster and so on. Fears of everything connected with nuclear power were blown up completely out of perspective with other risks. Hitler's man, Goebbles, had shown what propaganda could do, but the nuclear scientists never believed that it could succeed against the rationalism of science; yet succeed it did. The victory of the anti-nuclear activists was complete.

The anti-nuclear activists have won the battle, and to the victims belong the spoils: the failure of nuclear science to provide the cheap and abundant energy we need. This is the goal they cherished and they have achieved it. Our children and our grandchildren will be the victims of their heartless tactics.[4]

The campaign was led by left-wing politicians and supported financially by the Soviet Union.[5] The campaign was extraordinarily successful, and

---

[4] Bernard L. Cohen, *Nuclear Science and Society* (New York: Anchor Books, 1974).

[5] Many people are surprised and shocked when they are told this. The evidence is now available in *The Sword and the Shield: The Mitrokhin Archives and the Secret History of the KGB* by Christopher Andrew and Vasili Mitrokhin (New York: Basic Books, 1999; London: Penguin, 2000). Further evidence is provided by speakers at the conference mentioned in note 4 above.

gradually the public was turned against nuclear power, and it remains so until the present day. Those writing against nuclear power could pose as righteous and concerned citizens who were warning society against serious dangers, and so they were joined by many good and well-meaning people who did not realise that they were being used. More and more people became convinced of the evils of nuclear power, and the mass media were filled with antinuclear stories. Scientists who tried vainly to inject some objective facts were brushed aside by people whose ignorance is equalled only by their discourtesy.[6]

Strong support for the antinuclear campaign was provided by members of campaigns advocating nuclear disarmament, another Soviet campaign designed to render the West defenceless. They were convinced that anything nuclear is bad, and so when the Soviet Union collapsed and the cold war ended, they willingly joined the campaign against nuclear power stations. They were joined by those who see our technological society as evil.

An example of a good action that supported the campaign is provided by the 'children of Chernobyl' who were brought to the West to improve their health. They were advertised as suffering from nuclear radiation sickness and would die young and so naturally attracted much sympathy. In fact they were suffering from prolonged malnutrition and poor health care and not from radiation sickness. Pictures of heroic dying babies were used to solicit contributions to the cause.

It was seldom mentioned that the Soviet Union, recognising the value of nuclear power, was feverishly building their own nuclear power stations, designed to produce weapons-grade plutonium as well as power. The stations were so badly designed, so hurriedly built, and so badly managed that the disaster of Chernobyl was almost inevitable. Socialist nuclear power stations were, of course, good; it was only capitalist nuclear power stations that were bad.

---

[6] An example is provided by the member of parliament mentioned in my book *Nuclear Power, Energy and the Environment*, 161–62, and others appear in P. E. Hodgson, "Truth and Propaganda," *St Austin Review* (March/April 2004): 45 and "Reply to Mrs. Hawkins," (September/October 2004): 43.

The Church and Nuclear Power 145

## The Church and Nuclear Power

The Christian churches recognised the moral dimensions of the universal need for energy and in particular the question whether this could be satisfied by nuclear power, and many set up committees to study the subject and to make recommendations. In this article only the work of the Catholic Church will be considered,[7] with particular reference to the situation in Britain.

As early as 1980 the Pontifical Academy of Sciences arranged a study week and invited distinguished scientists from many countries to participate. After a week of discussions, they prepared a summary of their deliberations, which was duly published in a volume of 770 pages.[8] It is useful to recall their final conclusions:

> We have no time to waste. Energy policies are urgently needed, involving concerted action by the responsible bodies, and this requires the support of public opinion and energy users. Unfortunately, even in the industrialised countries, the public consciousness of the problem is lacking. . . . Only coal and nuclear power—together with a strong energy conservation policy and continued gas and oil exploration—can allow us to effectively meet the additional needs for the next two decades.

It is noteworthy that the Pontifical Academy understood clearly that when tackling such complex scientific and technological problems it is essential that its statements are based on careful study by well-qualified scientists who are experts in the relevant disciplines. They therefore produced an excellent and highly authoritative document that is still worth reading. Nearly all other Church statements were prepared by well-meaning people who failed to realise that expert

---

[7] A summary of statements by other churches is given in my review 'The Churches and Nuclear Power', August 1984 (unpublished). It is noteworthy that the bishops of the United States issued a document on some of the problems of the energy crisis. See my article, "Reflections on the Energy Crisis," in *Month* (November 1982): 382.

[8] André Blanc-Lapierre, ed., *Semaine d'étude sur le thème Humanité et énergie: Besoins—ressources—espoirs.* 10–15 November 1980. Pontificiae Academiae Scientiarum scripta varia, no. 46 (Città del Vaticano: Pontificia Academia Scientiarum, 1981).

knowledge is essential, and as a result produced statements that at best were banal and vacuous, and at worst positively misleading.

Subsequently, the report of the Pontifical Academy was given additional weight by being presented as the contribution of the Holy See to the Conference on Energy held in Vienna on 13–17 September 1982.[9] The leader of the Vatican delegation, Mgr Peressin, referred to the peaceful application of atomic energy, including in food conservation, new techniques of plant breeding, medicine, hydrology, and, most important of all, energy for industrial and private use. He reminded the conference that many United Nations agencies have stressed that the economic growth of the third world countries seems 'to be impossible without some applications of nuclear energy'. Therefore, Mgr Peressin continued, 'my delegation believes that all possible efforts should be made to extend to all countries, especially the developing ones, the benefits contained in the peaceful uses of nuclear energy'.

This highly authoritative work of the Pontifical Academy was a magnificent initiative that provided the scientific and technological data for the Church to take a leading part in working toward the solution of the world's energy problems. It is sad to relate that it has been almost entirely ignored.[10]

In the following years, the problems of the environment and global warming, already discussed at the meeting of the Pontifical Academy, became increasingly important. Several large international conferences, such as those at Rio and Kyoto, were convened to discuss these problems, and many nations pledged to reduce their emissions of carbon dioxide. It became clear that there is an urgent need to reduce the use of the fossil fuels, coal, oil, and natural gas. This is in any case an ultimate necessity because the natural resources are finite, though they are expected to last longer than was at one time feared.

---

[9] Statement of the Holy See to the International Conference on Nuclear Power, Vienna, 13–17 September 1982. International Atomic Energy Agency, Paper CN-42/449.

[10] During a lecture at the Gregorian University in Rome in 2002, I asked anyone who has heard of this document to raise his hand. In a large audience, not a single hand was raised.

The problem is then to find a way of generating enough electricity to satisfy our needs and to extend its benefits to the poorer countries. The success of the antinuclear campaign ensures that nuclear power is still unacceptable to many people, and so governments, terrified of losing votes, dare not take the obvious course of building nuclear power stations. Instead, they propose a great increase in what are called the 'benign renewables'—wind, solar, wave, tidal, and geothermal power. Hydropower cannot be much increased due to the limited availability of suitable rivers. However desirable the use of renewables may seem, the uncomfortable fact is that even wind power, the most promising renewable source, is unreliable, costly, relatively dangerous, and harmful to the environment. Whether we like it or not, it is just fantasy to suppose that we can meet our energy needs in this way.

The British government has organised meetings on the problem of global warming, and various possibilities were discussed, including energy conservation, increased taxes to reduce energy demand, and the expansion of the contribution of renewables. For political reasons, there was no mention of nuclear power, although that is demonstrably the only way to effect substantial reductions in carbon dioxide emissions.

The Church has also considered the problems of the environment and global warming, and the Bishops' Conference of England and Wales issued a statement entitled 'The Call of Creation'.[11] This said many valuable things, but there was no mention of nuclear power. A subsequent conference held at Belmont Abbey in February 2004, 'Faith and the Environmental Imperative', was somewhat better in that nuclear power was mentioned, and there was a strong statement in favour of nuclear power by retired Anglican bishop John Oliver.[12]

---

[11] The Department of International Affairs of the Catholic Bishops' Conference of England and Wales, *The Call of Creation* (London: Catholic Communications Service, 2002). The name of the author is not given on the booklet itself, but it is known to be Sr Denise Calder. A commentary on this booklet is published in the *St Austin Review* (November 2002): 31. The secrecy surrounding the authors of the bishops' statement prevents both fruitful dialogue and objective assessment of the qualifications of the author.

[12] 'Faith and the Environmental Imperative: Responding to "The Call of Creation": An Ecumenical Conference' at Belmont Abbey, Hereford, 21 February

The case for nuclear power, always overwhelming, has recently been further strengthened by a number of statements by respected authorities. Thus Lord May, the president of the Royal Society and formerly chief scientific advisor to the government, has written an article titled 'We Need More Nuclear Power Stations, Not Wishful Thinking'.[13] Professor James Lovelock, a distinguished scientist revered by environmentalists, has also come out strongly in favour of nuclear power in an article titled 'Only Nuclear Power Can Now Halt Global Warming'.[14] Even the *Tablet*, after publishing antinuclear articles for decades, published an article by Anglican bishop Hugh Montefiore strongly supporting nuclear power as the only practicable solution to our energy and global warming problems.[15] It retained its reputation, however, by subsequently publishing a typically ill-informed article and letter expressing a contrary view.

## Conclusion

The present situation is extremely unsatisfactory. It is obvious what has to be done, but such is the continuing influence of the Soviet antinuclear campaign that most people remain opposed to nuclear power. Governments are therefore unwilling to take the obvious decisions for fear of losing votes. Since energy policies have to be decided at least a decade ahead, it would seem desirable that they be decided by an all-party committee, thus ensuring that unpopular but necessary decisions do not adversely affect one party more than another.

The results of this indecision are beginning to appear. California, hardly a third world country, pinned its hopes on massively subsidised wind farms and built no other power stations. As a result, it has experienced power cuts and was forced to import electricity generated by

2004. A commentary on the conference is given in my article 'Flickers of Sanity', published in the *St Austin Review* (November/December 2004): 33. *See also* chapter 22, p. 109.

13 Lord May, 'We Need More Nuclear Power Stations, Not Wishful Thinking', *Daily Telegraph* (15 September 2004): 22.

14 James Lovelock, 'Only Nuclear Power Can Now Halt Global Warming', *Independent* (24 May 2004): 1.

15 Hugh Montefiore, 'Why the Planet Needs Nuclear Energy', *Tablet* (23 October 2004): 4.

nuclear power from neighbouring states. The price of oil has risen steeply, though largely for political reasons, but it is likely to remain high, together with that of natural gas. In Britain, the amount of spare generating capacity has been steadily falling and is now dangerously low. If there is a severe winter, power cuts are likely, and this will begin to bring home to the government the magnitude of its folly. One may then expect a public demand for nuclear power to save the situation, but it will be too late.

A possible strategy for the government is to say that it is necessary to build nuclear power stations now, because of the urgent need to sustain our power supplies. At the same time, the government should encourage the building of renewable sources and promise that as soon as the renewables prove reliable and less costly than the nuclear power stations, they would become our main power source, and the nuclear power stations would be decommissioned. This would challenge the supporters of the renewables to do their best to prove themselves, although many may believe that they can never succeed.

The Church has a great opportunity in this situation. The bishops are not constrained like the politicians and have the duty to speak out in a matter of such public concern. It is not only the responsibility of the bishops, for all other members of the Church have a similar responsibility to speak out. Rome gave a magnificent lead by emphasising as long as twenty-four years ago the need for urgent action. In spite of this, no further statement on nuclear power has been made by the bishops since the statement in *Briefing* in 1978. The Catholic press has, with very few exceptions, followed the Soviet antinuclear line.[16]

It is difficult not to conclude that a great opportunity to make a vital contribution to the future of our society has been lost. All the bishops had to do was to listen to Rome, and then to speak out. Not for the first time in history Rome was first, and then forgotten.

---

[16] The most notable exception is the *Month*, especially when edited by Mr Hugh Kay. The *Clergy Review* and *New Blackfriars* have also published the occasional article.

# PART IV
# Modern Physics

# CHAPTER 29

# A Tribute to Einstein*

## Relativity and the Absolutes

TO THOSE WHO WORK in the field of physics the news of the death of Albert Einstein comes like the loss of a personal friend; to the rest he is a mysterious figure, almost a symbol of the seeming incomprehensibility of modern science. His name will be forever linked with the theory of relativity, yet even if he had never written a line on relativity he would have been remembered as long as physics lasts. His great year was in 1905, when, at the age of twenty-six he published three papers—on the special theory of relativity, the photoelectric effect, and the Brownian movement—each bringing order and clarity where before there was chaos and confusion, and each enough to establish an international reputation. His scientific work is characterised by a directness of approach that goes straight to the heart of a problem and lays bare its essential simplicity. In his autobiography, he recalled the awakening of his sense of wonder at nature when his father showed him a compass needle for the first time at the age of four or five. This experience filled him with the conviction that something deeply hidden lies behind things. He was inspired a second time in a different way by the apparently inexorable logic of Euclid, and much of his work is an attempt to understand what lies behind things by means of geometrical analogies.

---

* Peter Hodgson, "A Tribute to Einstein," *Tablet* (23 April 1995): 205, 392.

This is particularly so for the theory of relativity, which provided an elegant solution to many difficulties that had been accumulating in the previous decades. It was, of course, not entirely his creation; he derived many essential ideas from his predecessors, especially Poincaré, Lorentz, and Mach. It marked a fundamental turning point in the development of physics. Previously, in the Newtonian synthesis that had reigned supreme for two centuries, it had been taken for granted that man has a fundamental intuition of the nature of space and time that can be used to build his science. But this is not so, and Einstein, following Mach, recognised that space and time for the physicist are defined by the operations used to measure them and that any theory on which they appear must simply take these operations into account. Thus modern science looks at nature from the viewpoint of a man and not from that of an angel. Perhaps this has contributed to the humility of contemporary scientists compared with the confident dogmatism of a century ago.

For some reason relativity captured the public imagination. People were soon applying it to the most diverse subjects and speaking of relativity in morals and law. Philosophers understanding nothing of the scientific theory wrote eloquent books showing how it proved their pet theories. Einstein was condemned as an atheist and as a religious idealist. All this was most regrettable and would probably have been avoided if the theory had been called the theory of absolutes, since its main point is to exclude what is relative and formulate the laws of nature in an invariant form. It is related that the archbishop of Canterbury asked Einstein to explain the relevance of relativity to religion. Einstein replied simply, 'None. Relativity is a purely scientific matter and has nothing to do with religion.'

Before Einstein, a natural phenomenon was considered to be explained if a mechanical model of it could be constructed and its course calculated by the application of Newton's laws to the model. This finally broke down in the latter half of the 19th century when repeated attempts to construct a mechanical model of the ether failed. But now physicists realise that there is no reason to suppose that such mechanical models can be made, and they are content with mathematical equations alone. This approach to science, intimately linked with the rise of the logical positivist movement, has certainly increased the economy of scientific thought, but there is reason to believe that now it is hindering progress by discouraging attempts to discover the more fundamental processes underlying the apparently statistical nature of atomic and nuclear phenomena. Einstein has resolutely opposed this tendency, declaring that such processes will be discovered, just as laws of motion for the individual molecules were found to underlie the statistical laws governing the behaviour of gases. He summed this up vividly when he said he refused to believe in a God who played dice with nature.

We are, of course, far too close to him to attempt any final evaluation of his works, but it is certain that he will ever be counted among the greatest scientists of all time.

But what of Einstein the man? He was no cold ivory-tower scientist but a very humble, kind, and lovable person. He was a true humanist and said that 'concern for man himself and his fate must always form the chief interest of all technical endeavours. . . . Never forget this in the midst of your diagrams and equations.' Yet he had no exaggerated conception of the place of the scientist in society, saying that 'the intellectual workers cannot successfully intervene directly in the political struggle. They can achieve, however, the spreading of clear ideas about the situation and the possibility of successful action. They can contribute through enlightenment to prevent able statesmen from being hampered in their work by antiquated opinions and prejudices.'

He hated restraints on the freedom of the individual and the folly and futility of war and readily, sometimes too readily, allowed his name to be used by organizations formed to combat them. Yet he signed the letter of 2 August 1939, written by American scientists to President Roosevelt, warning him of the military possibilities of atomic energy and urging that the American government undertake an extensive research programme. It was doubly appropriate that he should do this; not only was he the most distinguished and respected scientist in the country, but his work on the transformation of mass into energy underlies the newly discovered source of energy. In subsequent years he again and again protested attacks on human freedom. On the Oppenheimer case, for example, he wrote, 'The systematic and widespread attempt to destroy mutual trust and confidence constitutes the severest possible blow against society'.

He spent the last years of his life quietly working at the Princeton Institute for Advanced Study, surrounded by some of the most brilliant researchers in the world, and was loved and respected by them all. Many anecdotes are told of his later years. One tells of a small girl who, hearing that a great mathematician lived next door, went to him for help with her homework. She returned home and told her mother that the kind man had made it all much clearer than the teacher. The mother called to apologize for her daughter's intrusion, but Einstein said that on the contrary he had been delighted by the visit. It is also said that he was a well-known figure in the streets of Princeton, ambling along in baggy trousers and pullover and, as often as not, with complete unselfconsciousness, contentedly licking an ice cream.

# CHAPTER 30

# Can God Intervene through Quantum Events?

WE BELIEVE that we are all totally dependent on God: He cares for us and guides our lives. We also believe that scientific research has shown that the natural world behaves according to strict laws that admit no exception; it is like a vast machine. How, then, can God act on the world?

It has been suggested that the new physics provides an answer to this question. Quantum mechanics, it is argued, shows the 'cloudy and fitful' nature of the microworld. Since according to this view the microworld is not strictly determined, like the world of classical physics, 'quantum theory seems to leave room for God to affect the outcomes of physical processes' by actions on the microworld within the limits of quantum indeterminacy and without violating the laws of physics. 'Given billions and billions of such minute interventions, God might be able to effect significant changes on the macroscopic level'. Indeed, one might not need so many interventions since chaos theory has shown the extreme sensitivity of dynamical processes to minute changes in the initial conditions. Schrödinger's cat is a familiar example of a single quantum event producing a macroscopic event.

This explanation of God's action on the world relies on the indeterminate character of the microworld. The key question is whether quantum outcomes 'are essentially indeterminate in nature' without any determinate substratum. If we examine the experimental study of quantum events, we find that observations and measurements of microworld phenomena always concern individual events. We observe a photon emitted from an excited atom when it impinges on a counter or photographic plate. Similarly we observe an alpha particle emitted from a radioactive source at a particular time, or a particle scattered by a nucleus in a particular direction.

We cannot use quantum mechanics to calculate these individual events. We cannot calculate the time of emission of a photon or an alpha particle nor the direction in which a particle is scattered. Quantum mechanics enables us to calculate only the probability of emission or the probability of scattering in a particular direction. Knowing this, we allow our counts to accumulate until we know these probabilities to the desired accuracy.

Since quantum mechanics gives only probabilities, it is an essentially statistical theory. Thus when it is said that the microworld is irreducibly statistical, it is being implicitly assumed that quantum mechanics gives a complete account of the world. This can be said only by one who is looking at the world as described by quantum mechanics, not at the world itself, a world of particular events.

Since quantum mechanics is unable to provide the means to calculate the details of individual events, it is an incomplete theory. This was denied by Bohr, who held that quantum mechanics is the end of the road for physics and that no improvement is possible. It is the last, the final, the never-to-be-surpassed revolution in physics. Karl Popper regarded this claim as outrageous.

The indeterminacy of the microworld is often illustrated by the Heisenberg uncertainty principle. It is well known that if a beam of electrons passes through a narrow slit, the width of the resulting diffraction pattern varies inversely as the width of the slit. If the width of the slit is the uncertainty in position $\Delta x$ and that of the diffraction pattern is the uncertainty in transverse momentum $\Delta p$, then $\Delta x \Delta p > h/4\pi$, where $h$ is Planck's constant. The more accurately we know the position, the less we know about the momentum, and vice versa. This is interpreted to mean that these variables are inherently fuzzy, that an electron has no definite position and momentum or that precise knowledge of this sort will never be possible. It can easily be seen that this is incorrect, because we can put a second slit in the screen receiving the electrons and thus determine the transverse momentum of electrons passing through this second slit with far greater accuracy than that specified by the uncertainty principle. Even if we could not do this, it is illegitimate to argue from our inability to measure something exactly that it does not exist exactly. The uncertainty principle is thus a statistical statement about a large number of electrons and should not be applied to a single electron. The statistical interpretation of quantum mechanics resolves the quantum paradoxes, such as those associated with the wave-particle duality, the collapse of the wave function, radioactive decay, and the double slit.

The incompleteness of quantum mechanics was also shown by Einstein, Podolsky, and Rosen. They imagined a particle breaking into two equal parts that fly off in opposite directions. It is then possible to measure the position of one particle to any desired accuracy, and similarly the momentum of the other. Since by the conservation of momentum each particle has the same velocity, any measurement made on one immediately gives the corresponding quantity for the other, and so we have a way to measure both the position and the momentum of a particle to any desired accuracy, contrary to the Heisenberg uncertainty principle.

Statistical theories are familiar in classical physics. Thus the kinetic theory of gases enables us to calculate the values of macroscopic variables like temperature and pressure by taking statistical averages over the variables describing the motions of the constituent molecules, which are unknown. No one doubts that each molecule has a definite trajectory and a position and velocity at any instant of time, yet there are so many particles that a complete calculation of their motions would be impossible. Thus statistical behaviour at one level does not exclude a fully deterministic substratum. The question is, then, whether quantum mechanics has such a substratum, specified by the so-called hidden variables. The mathematician von Neumann analysed the situation mathematically and concluded that there could be no hidden variables in quantum mechanics, but this was refuted by Bohm, who constructed a hidden variable theory, and by Bell, who found the unjustified assumption in von Neumann's proof. There is thus no reason to believe that there are no such hidden variables.

There are several ways of thinking about the microworld in a deterministic way. One of these is the pilot wave theory, first proposed by de Broglie and later on developed by Bohm. According to this theory, the Schrödinger equation describes a wave that guides the motion of the particle. Another is called stochastic electrodynamics, which takes account of the fluctuating electromagnetic radiation that forms the background to all quantum phenomena.

It is sometimes suggested that it was only Einstein in his old age who defended a deterministic theory of quantum mechanics. In his book *The God of Chance*, Bartholomew remarks that 'a minority' of physicists hold that 'it would ultimately be possible to construct a theory of matter in which all uncertainty is removed'. He lists Einstein, Planck, de Broglie, and Bohm among them. He could have added Dirac, Schrödinger, Fermi, and Feynman. Hardly a negligible group.

It is possible that further research will establish one of these theories. It may well be, however, that because the determinate nature of the microworld is itself inherently statistical, these may not make any predictions that can be tested experimentally. Physicists will take no notice of the new theories until they give predictions different from those of quantum mechanics and until these predictions are verified experimentally. At present it seems rather unlikely that this will happen, and so quantum mechanics may in practice remain the final theory. It is, however, important to recognise that it remains a statistical theory, and this will save us from being confused by quantum paradoxes and all the other unjustified conclusions that have been deduced from them.

The quantum world, like the classical world, has many features that we do not understand, even if we can describe them mathematically, and this must be clearly distinguished from the illogicality of quantum paradoxes.

The foregoing has shown that the success of quantum mechanics does not imply that the world is indeterminate and so does not provide the means whereby God can intervene. Even if it did, such interventions would not be able to account for all recorded interventions, since they violate other physical principles. Quantum mechanics, as Einstein remarked, is but one step along the long road of our attempts to understand the natural world. We need always to be humble before the complexities of nature and to leave open the way to deeper understanding.

# CHAPTER 31

# God and the Quantum World[*]

THE QUANTUM NATURE of the physical world was discovered by Max Planck in the early years of the 20th century. He was studying thermodynamics, and his attention was drawn to the frequency distribution of the black-body radiation. This radiation is emitted from a small hole in a heated enclosure with rough walls that ensure that radiation reaches statistical equilibrium before emission. The frequency distribution is found to be independent of the material lining the walls of the oven, so Planck realised that it must be a fundamental characteristic of all matter. This frequency distribution had been measured by several experimentalists, and Planck resolved to try to see how it can be derived theoretically.

Already Rayleigh and Jeans had used classical radiation theory to derive an expression that fitted the data well at low frequencies but tended to infinity at high frequencies, which was of course unacceptable. The physicist Wien had derived a formula that fitted the data at high frequencies but failed at low frequencies.

Planck used an ingenious argument based on entropy to interpolate between these two formulae and obtained a formula, now known as the Planck distribution, that fitted the data perfectly. Now his task was to understand the physics behind his formula. He used the familiar

---

* References to the original papers and further discussion may be found in Peter Hodgson, "God's Action in the World: Relevance of Quantum Mechanics," *Zygon* 35 (September 2000): 505.

technique of assuming that the energy is emitted in small finite amounts, and then he let their size tend to zero, so as to represent a continuous distribution. To his great surprise, the intermediate formula with discrete amounts of energy, called quanta, gave the Planck distribution, but the final result, with infinitely small quanta, did not.

All his instincts as a physicist rebelled against this result. Surely energy must be emitted continuously. He tried hard to find a way to avoid this unwelcome conclusion but without success. He had to admit that it is a feature of the world. Soon it was confirmed by Einstein's interpretation of the photoelectric effect.

This story shows clearly that physicists do not impose their ideas on the world but recognise and accept what they find, whether or not it agrees with their original ideas. The world is made by God in ways that often we cannot imagine.

A few years later Rutherford discovered that the atom has a small central nucleus with most of the mass, with a number of electrons around it. Bohr used the idea of the quantum to build his model of the atom. He assumed that the electrons go around the nucleus in discrete orbits and that radiation is emitted when an electron falls from one orbit to a lower one. With this model, he was able to calculate to high accuracy the frequencies of the radiation emitted from an excited hydrogen atom. This was a great achievement, but to get his result, he had to assume that the electrons stayed in their orbit, whereas classical theory predicted that they would continuously lose energy and rapidly spiral into the nucleus.

These problems were solved by the development of quantum mechanics in the 1920s by Heisenberg, Schrödinger, Dirac, and others. This enabled what is called the wave function to be calculated for any physical system, and from the wave function the probabilities of measurable quantities. It is a beautiful theory, but is difficult to understand physically.

Bohr and Heisenberg developed what is called the Copenhagen interpretation, which maintains that the wave function contains all that can be known about each particular quantum system. A consequence is that it is not possible, for example, to measure both the position and the momentum of a particle; the more accurately we know one of them, the less accurately we know the other. This is the Heisenberg uncertainty relation, and it has been taken to imply that the world is fuzzy and indeterminate. Also, it seems that electrons sometimes behave like a wave and sometimes like a particle.

This fuzzy nature of the world has been used in an attempt to solve an outstanding problem about God's action in the world. According to classical physics, the world is a completely determined system. How, then, can God act on the world in answer to our prayers? Similarly, we believe that we have free will, but how do we act on the world? The suggestion now is that God acts on the world within the limits of the uncertainty principle and thus does not go against the laws of physics. To the objection that such tiny intervention cannot cause large-scale effects, we can reply that chaos theory has taught us that very small changes to many physical systems can have very large effects.

These and similar suggestions have led to much discussion, both theological and physical. First, is God bound by His own laws? Surely He is Lord of nature and can override or suspend His laws at will. Furthermore, there are many instances of His intervention, such as some of those recorded in the Gospels and in modern centres of healing that cannot be explained in this way, as they contradict the conservation of matter.

Second, there are other ways of interpreting quantum mechanics. Einstein always opposed the Copenhagen interpretation, emphasising that the wave function describes the average behaviour of an ensemble of similar systems, not each particular system. It is often said that quantum mechanics enables us to calculate any observable quantity, but this is not so. For example, I can record the time at which a particular radioactive nucleus decays, but I cannot calculate it by quantum mechanics. What I can calculate, and this is of course very useful, is the probability that it will decay in a certain time interval. All quantum mechanical calculations are of this character.

Looking at things in this way removes what are sometimes called the mysteries of the quantum world. The Heisenberg uncertainty principle refers to the distributions of positions and momenta; each individual electron is a particle with a definite position and momentum. The probability distribution of an ensemble of electrons obeys a wave equation, but this does not imply that electrons are waves. The wave-particle dilemma is thus a category confusion, similar to that between the actual duration of the life of an individual and his statistical life expectancy.

Another problem that has been used to illustrate the strangeness of the quantum world is the double-slit experiment. A beam of electrons of the same energy is directed at a screen with two closely spaced, narrow parallel slits. The electrons pass through the slits and are recorded on a screen beyond the slits. Detectors at the second screen show what is called an interference pattern. If we close one of the slits, electrons can pass only through the other slit, and we find a diffraction pattern on the screen, and similarly for the other slit. If electrons are particles, each electron must pass through one slit or the other, so when both slits are open we would expect to find a superposition of two diffraction patterns, but instead, we find an interference pattern. It seems that an electron going through one slit knows whether or not the other slit is open. How can we understand this? Could it be that the electrons going through one slit interfere with the electrons going through the other slit? No, because the experiment can be done with a beam of such low intensity that only one electron is passing through the apparatus at a time. Could an electron divide into two and interfere with itself? No, because many experiments show that an electron behaves like a point particle down to an extremely small distance, at most $10^{-15}$ of a centimetre, which is far smaller than the slit size.

A possible explanation is that opening or shutting a slit affects the field, possibly the electromagnetic field, in the vicinity of the other slit. In this way the electron knows whether the other slit is open or not. This possibility is discussed in more detail below.

According to the Copenhagen interpretation, quantum mechanics is the end of the road, the final never-to-be-surpassed theory of the physical world. If this is so, there is no hope that the paradoxes of the quantum world will ever be resolved. Opponents of the Copenhagen interpretation hoped that someday there would be found what they called 'hidden variables' that determine the course of phenomena. Averages over these hidden variables would then give the observed quantum mechanical statistical distribution, in the same way that averages over the motions of gas molecules give the thermodynamical variables, such as pressure and temperature. This hope was dashed in the 1930s, when the very eminent mathematician John von Neumann showed that it is not possible to find a deterministic theory in terms of hidden variables that underpins the statistical nature of the quantum world. As a result, the Copenhagen interpretation was adopted by most physicists.

However, in 1952 David Bohm published a new interpretation of quantum mechanics in terms of hidden variables. He did what von Neumann had shown to be impossible. A few years later the puzzle was solved by John Bell, who found the flaw in von Neumann's reasoning. Like all mathematical proofs, it relied on various assumptions, and one of them, though very reasonable, was in fact false. Some types of hidden variables were not excluded by von Neumann's proof, and so the way to a deeper understanding was open again.

The possibility of this deeper understanding is the hallmark of Einstein's view of quantum mechanics. To him, it is not the final theory but one step on a long road. There have been several attempts to make a deeper theory, and among these it is useful to consider the pilot wave theory of de Broglie and Bohm and stochastic electrodynamics.

The pilot wave theory considers the electron as a particle whose motion is guided by a wave. This is formulated mathematically and enables the trajectories of the electrons to be calculated. This has been done for reflection by a potential barrier and for the double-slit experiment. This shows very clearly how the individual trajectories together form the observed interference pattern. Many people, however, find this theory unsatisfactory because it fails to give a physical picture of what is going on.

The second theory, quantum electrodynamics, is more attractive, as it gives such a physical picture. It starts from the observation that every hydrogen atom, for example, is not totally isolated (as is assumed in the textbook calculations of its structure) but is continually bathed in electromagnetic radiation from the surrounding atoms. In classical mechanics such external forces are small or can be allowed for, but in the atomic and nuclear domains they are large and are taken into account by the quantum mechanical formalism. The picture we now have of the hydrogen atom is that the electrons are hit by the photons of this electromagnetic radiation and move around the nucleus in a zigzag path so that their probability distribution is just what is given by a quantum mechanical calculation.

This theory has been formulated mathematically and has been shown to give exactly the same results as quantum mechanics for the simple case of the harmonic oscillator. Unfortunately more realistic problems raise great mathematical difficulties. In some cases it has been shown that stochastic electrodynamics and quantum mechanics give different predictions, but the requisite experiments have not yet been done. When they are done, they should provide a decisive test of the theory.

These two examples show that research is actively continuing to find the deeper structure of the quantum world. There is much hard work to be done, and it should reveal more clearly the detailed structure of the atomic and nuclear world. This continual dialectic between theory and experiment is characteristic of scientific research, and as one theory supersedes another, it shows how unwise it is to base theological conclusions on the latest theory.

The Copenhagen interpretation is still held by many physicists, although they do not follow it in practice. It is ultimately based on a positivistic view of the world that will not admit into a theory anything that cannot be measured or observed. However, many scientists have said most strongly that it is valuable to postulate unobservables, for very often what is unobservable at one time becomes observable later. In philosophical circles, realism is now superseding positivism.

Einstein was not a lone figure opposing the pioneers Bohr, Heisenberg, and Pauli. His view was supported in one way and another by Planck, de Broglie, Schrödinger, Dirac, and Feynman.

As a final example of the presumed interaction of theology and quantum mechanics, there are some who seek an understanding of the dual nature of Christ, who is both God and man, by considering the dual nature of the electron, which is both a wave and a particle. We cannot understand the dual nature of the electron, but we accept it, so why should we not also accept the dual nature of Christ? Enough has been said to show the fallacy in this argument. The electron is a particle, and the so-called wave behaviour appears only when we consider the behaviour of a large number of electrons. It is thus a mistake to say that a single electron shows wave behaviour. Furthermore, as mentioned, the wave behaviour is shown by the motions of a large number of electrons acting individually, with no mutual interactions. This is quite unlike the waves we encounter in everyday life, which are the cooperative behaviour of a large number of molecules acting together. Thus all we can say is that an ensemble of electrons behaves in a way that follows the same equation as the waves of everyday experience. It is possible for quite different phenomena to obey the same equation, so it is only by analogy that we use the term 'wave' when we speak of the behaviour of electrons.

Theologians find it useful to distinguish between God's primary and secondary causality. By His primary causality, He is the Creator of all that is and continually sustains it in being. In addition, by His secondary causality, he gives created beings specific natures so that they normally behave exactly in accord with their natures. It is this behaviour that is the subject of scientific research. Thus we say that the natures of hydrogen and oxygen are such that they combine to form water. If we deny secondary causality, we would say, with the Muslims, that when hydrogen and oxygen come together, then Allah creates water. This shows the importance of theology in providing the basis of science.

It is thus possible, following Einstein, to maintain that the world is a determined system following exactly the laws given to it by God. It is hazardous to use the theories of modern physics to solve theological difficulties.

# CHAPTER 32

# Time*

A TRAVELLER from abroad, wishing to know the time but being unfamiliar with English idioms, asked a passerby, 'What is time, please?' He was disconcerted by the reply: 'That is a very profound philosophical question'. Of course we all know what time is, until we are asked. St Augustine has some very profound things to say about time, which are still frequently quoted, but even he could not say what time is.

This ignorance about the nature of time does not stop us from measuring it very accurately. Many times each day we look at our watches as we hurry from one appointment to the next. Compared with people long ago, who lived comparatively relaxed lives, we surround ourselves with labour-saving (and therefore time-saving) devices. With our computer we can do calculations in a fraction of a second that previously would have taken years. We have machines to wash our clothes and dishes, shave our faces, and even brush our teeth, yet what do we do with the time we save? We continue to work frantically to earn more money to buy more time-saving devices. Kipling sternly reminded us that 'if you can fill the unforgiving minute with sixty seconds, worth of distance run, then yours is the earth and everything in it'. He could be answered by the reflection, 'What does it profit a man to gain the whole world and suffer the loss of his soul?'

---

* Peter Hodgson, "Time," *Catholic Herald* (17 April 2003): 10.

We jealously guard our time and behave as if it all belongs to us. We don't like to be interrupted or forced to waste our time. We talk about 'spending' time, as if it were our own money. We are quite wrong about this; in reality all our time belongs to God.

God is timeless. When Gerontius died, he 'heard no more the busy beat of time'. 'Be still and know that I am God', Psalm 46 reminds us. There is a Jewish Hasidim saying, 'Where there is a clock there is no soul'. We need to stop rushing around and sit quietly until our thoughts are stilled. People who have done this say that their minds become clear and they can then see what is really important in their lives and what is just useless activity. They realise that decisions taken in a hurry are nearly always wrong.

The churches of the East have a much more relaxed sense of time. There were no clocks in the monasteries of Mount Athos until the 18th century, and even then they were imported from the West. In contrast, the Western monasteries had highly sophisticated clocks as early as the 14th century. Perhaps this different attitude toward time accounts for the rise of modern science in the West but not in the East.

Seeking quietness and serenity in our personal lives does not mean that we should inconvenience others. Our modern world would soon become chaotic if nobody bothered about time. It is a sign of humility, of respect, and of concern for others to arrive on time, as it is a duty of those responsible for transport to ensure that buses, trains, and planes keep to their timetables. We can each remain quiet in ourselves, and, providing we start our journey in good time, we need not hurry.

I must stop here, as I have to hurry to catch the post.

# CHAPTER 33

# Creation from Nothing*

THERE IS NO greater difference, at the material level, than that between being and not-being, or between something and nothing. Only God can create being; that is, only He can cause something to exist where previously there was nothing. The transition from not-being to being is beyond the power of science to detect. It is impossible to show by scientific methods that there is nothing in a specified volume, because it is always possible that there is something present that cannot be detected by our existing instruments. A fortiori, it is impossible by scientific methods to detect the creation of everything, for before the creation there were no scientists or scientific instruments.

Once these fundamental truths are understood, it is easy to assess the casual and flippant statements made by popularisers of modern cosmology. Thus to say that the universe stumbled into being by accident through a chance fluctuation in the vacuum or that space-time formed itself out of its own dust is not only unwarranted speculation but is simply nonsense. Even if it is granted that a fluctuation in a vacuum could produce material objects, then such a 'vacuum' is rich in potentialities and so cannot properly be described as nothing.

There is a more sophisticated form of the argument that is worth discussing further. It has been remarked that the total gravitational

---

* Peter Hodgson, "Creation from Nothing," *Faith* (September/October 2004): 8.

potential of the universe is almost equal to the total mass, but of opposite sign. If they really are exactly equal, then the total energy of the universe is zero, and so creation could take place without violating the principle of the conservation of energy. Now consider the Heisenberg uncertainty principle in the form $\Delta E \Delta t > h$, where $h$ is Planck's constant. This principle says that we can violate energy conservation by an amount $\Delta E$, but only for a time $\Delta t$, and this is used in the theory of virtual particles. So if $E$ is the energy of the universe, then the universe can exist by a fluctuation in the vacuum for a time $\Delta t$, even if the total energy of the universe is not exactly zero. If $\Delta E$ is exceedingly small, then $\Delta t$ can be exceedingly large.

This speculation conflates two errors: first, the absolute distinction between being and not-being, and second, the application to a single system of the Heisenberg uncertainty principle, which, like all quantum mechanical statements, applies only to an ensemble of similar systems.

All that physical science can really establish, and of course this is exceedingly important, is that if there exists matter of specified properties, and if at a certain time it is in a specified state, then, provided nothing else interferes, it will change in time following certain differential equations. This was realised by Stephen Hawking, in a rare flash of metaphysical realism, when he asked, "What is it that breathes fire into the equations?"

The Christian beliefs concerning creation emphasise not only that the universe was created by God out of nothing and in time but also that the universe is totally dependent on God and totally distinct from God. That is, the universe at any instant is sustained in being by God, and without this sustaining power it would immediately lapse into nothingness. The universe is in no way an emanation from God or a part of God; this excludes all forms of pantheism, which was one of the beliefs preventing the rise of science in all ancient cultures. Pantheism is explicitly excluded by the belief that Christ is the only-begotten Son of God, that He was begotten, not made. Only Christ is begotten; the universe was made, not begotten. This is the connection between Christian belief, as expressed in the Nicene Creed (*Et in unum*

*Dominum Jesum Christum, Filium Dei unigenitum. . . . Genitum, non factum. . . .),* and the only viable birth of science in western Europe.

Also excluded by Christian belief is any form of dualism, any idea that the material world is the battleground between different spirits. To make this absolutely clear, all creation takes place through Christ *(per quem omnia facta sunt).*

Inherent in the Christian doctrine of creation is the belief that God freely chose to create the universe. He was not in any way constrained either to create or not to create it in the way that He did. It is therefore not a necessary universe in the sense that it had to be created or could not have been created otherwise. There is therefore no possibility of finding out about the universe by pure thought or by a priori reasoning. We can therefore only hope to understand it by studying it and by making experiments. Thus the Christian doctrine of creation encouraged the experimental method, essential for the development of science.

# CHAPTER 34

# Jesuits and the Green Flash

VERY OCCASIONALLY, just as the sun sets, there is a green flash. More precisely, the red or yellow rim of the setting sun is tinged with green, and as the sun sets, this green fringe becomes wider until at the instant of setting only the green remains. This effect was first noticed in ancient times, and there have been many speculations about its origin. The most obvious one is that it is just a physiological effect; when we have been looking at the redness of the setting sun, the retina becomes fatigued, and we see the complementary colour, which is green. This suggestion can be tested by photographing the effect, which is easier said than done because the green flash is very rarely seen. The difficulties have, however, been overcome by two Jesuits working at the Vatican Observatory, Fr D. J. K. O'Connell and Fr C. Treusch. They succeeded in photographing the green flash, and their photographs were published in a book in 1958. Another argument against the physiological effect theory is that the green flash is also observed around the time of sunrise, when the eye has not been exposed to the redness of the sun.

Depending on the time of year, the sun as seen from the Vatican Observatory sets either over the Tolfa Mountains or over the Mediterranean Sea. The Vatican photographs were taken at intervals of a few seconds and show the appearance of the sun's disk just before the sun sets. Most of the photographs were taken as the sun set behind mountains and show the characteristic sequence of a green rim gradually increasing as the sun dips below the horizon. One photograph shows the sun setting behind a cloud bank, with a rather indistinct green flash. Many fine details are revealed in the photographs, and it would not be possible to see them with the unaided eye.

It is even more difficult to see the green flash at sunrise because one does not know exactly where and when the sun will appear. In one of the Jesuit photographs the sun's disc appears white with a brilliant blue rim. Lord Kelvin once saw the blue flash at sunrise. In other photographs the green rim is seen first as the sun rises above the horizon, and then the remainder of the sun appears, still with the green rim. In a second or two the green is gone.

The green flash is also visible through a telescope when the planets Mars and Venus dip below the horizon. Several photographs of the green flash, observed as Venus sets, were obtained by the Jesuit astronomers and published in their book.

**Note:** For several years I have looked for the green flash during the summer as the sun sets over Cape Point in South Africa. On rare occasions it is clearly visible as a change in colour from yellow-orange to turquoise-blue of the two sides of the last tip of the sun just before it sets. As it sets they move together and merge just before the sun actually sets. Only once have I seen an actual flash of turquoise-blue light. It may be that the colour depends on the atmospheric conditions.

## Reference

D. J. K. O'Connell and C. Treusch, *The Green Flash and Other Low Sun Phenomena* (Amsterdam: North-Holland Publishing Co., 1958; New York: Interscience Publishing, 1958).

# PART V

# Philosophy of Science

## CHAPTER 35

# Hypothesis, Theory, and Certainty in the Physical Sciences

THE OVERRIDING AIM of the scientist is to understand as completely as possible the natural phenomena that interest him. The stages in his work have frequently been described in terms of the traditional categories of hypothesis, law, and theory, but this description, though containing some elements of truth, is now completely inadequate to describe the richness and complexity of modern scientific research. The old words are still used, but the meanings they bear have become greatly diversified and in particular cases do not correspond to the real status of their subject. Thus, for example, scientists still refer to Avogadro's hypothesis, though it is now one of the basic facts of chemistry. Physicists speak of Boyle's law, but this is now known to be only an approximate generalisation, and the deviations from it are well understood. The kinetic theory of gases underlying and explaining Boyle's law was originally a hypothesis, but now it is, at least in its central affirmation, simply a statement of fact. The theory of evolution, likewise, is now so extensively confirmed that it is essentially a factual statement insofar as it asserts that living organisms, as we know them, have developed over the ages; the detailed explanation of how this happened is, however, still a subject of theoretical speculation.

To see the precise significance of the words describing the methods and results of scientific research, it is thus necessary to examine in detail the development of scientific knowledge in different fields. Only in this way can the significance of particular generalisations be understood, together with the methods by which they can be verified and their progress from unsupported hypothesis to accepted fact. The examples discussed here are taken mainly from nuclear physics, one of the most fundamental branches of science. Nuclear physics deals with phenomena rather remote from our human experience, and thus it shows the method of science stretched to its furthest limits.

Before discussing some examples in detail, it is useful to summarise in a general way the stages of discovery and understanding that are common to all sciences. The first stage, the recognition that a particular phenomenon exists, requires an explanation. In the biological sciences, this stage is so obvious that it does not require any comment. We are surrounded by plants and animals, and the scientist naturally wants to understand their function and behaviour. He will of course seek to discover new species, but the real scientific work begins only with the detailed study of the physiology and ecology of each organism. In the physical sciences, on the other hand, the primary phenomena are frequently not evident to the unaided senses. In nuclear physics, for example, it may be necessary to make long and complicated experiments even to establish the existence of the particles that we study.

The recognition of phenomena is not always a matter of a detailed search in new realms of experience; it is often simply the recognition of the significance of phenomena that are quite familiar. We look at our surroundings in a new way, and a branch of science is born. It required great originality to see that Edinburgh Castle is built on the core of a long-extinct volcano, and this immediately leads to a dynamic concept of geology. Those placid mountains, apparently immutable, are the result of the interaction of mighty terrestrial forces, of continual changes, some gradual and some cataclysmic, over countless millions of years. Once the new insight is gained, it is irreversible; it becomes impossible to look at the phenomena in the old way again. It is a familiar experience that a scientific understanding, so hard to obtain, is afterward seen as almost obvious and inescapable. It is often the case that many obscure and difficult experiments lead to the new insight, but when we have it, we immediately see many simple experiments that easily lead to the same result.

The second stage in scientific investigation is the detailed measurement of the phenomena of interest. In biology, this corresponds to the dissection and anatomical investigation of the organism itself and to the way it depends on and interacts with its surroundings and with the members of the same species. In nuclear physics, the corresponding stage is the study of the formation, interaction, and decay of the particles concerned. In the range of the sciences, this work gives an immense body of factual data that demands a coherent and intelligible explanation. A collection of facts, as Poincaré remarked, is no more a science than a heap of stones is a house.

The third stage is the attempt to understand this factual data by means of hypotheses concerning the detailed mechanism underlying the appearances. Each hypothesis must be tested against the factual data and is acceptable only if it successfully accounts for it. Frequently the hypothesis will suggest new measurements that enable it to be subjected to a more severe test, and the new measurements may themselves reveal new phenomena. The scientist makes hypotheses continually, and the interaction between hypotheses and experiment, between fact and theory, is the very lifeblood of scientific investigation. The scientist does not wait until he has assembled all the factual information before he starts to make hypotheses to account for it. That would be stupid and wasteful, for the possible factual information, even in a small branch of science, is potentially infinite. His aim is rather to find just those essential facts that will lead him to a true understanding of the phenomena. There is of course a difficulty here, in that until he understands the phenomena, he does not know what facts are the most significant. So he has to proceed by a process of trial and error, iterating the partial understanding obtained by his preliminary hypotheses and their comparison with experiment until he has grasped the essentials of the phenomena. This process goes on continually at the frontier of science and leaves behind it an established body of knowledge at the same time as it reveals an ever-increasing field of phenomena that are still obscure. The scientist is thus at the same time conscious of the certainty of what he has established and the immensity of his ignorance.

As the third stage proceeds, the first tentative hypotheses are refined and generalised and, where possible, given precise mathematical formulation. In this stage the scientist frequently makes use of what he does understand to penetrate into the regions of ignorance. He draws analogies and makes conceptual models, and these may be either physical or mathematical. Sometimes these analogies are apparently contradictory on the physical level, like the wave and particle theories of light, but are reconciled when expressed in more general mathematical terms.

The early theories of the electromagnetic field were conceived in physical terms, as due to vibrations in an all-pervading ether. The Michelson-Morley experiment showed that this is untenable, and it became necessary to adopt a more austere formulation in terms of Maxwell's equations. The physical model thus served as a help to the investigation on the way to a more general theory. Maxwell's equations, in their turn, can be expressed more generally in the form of a field tensor that is invariant under the Lorentz transformation of special relativity. It is when the generalisations have reached this level that the fundamental unity of the physical sciences becomes particularly apparent. Completely diverse phenomena in the domains of light, electricity, and magnetism are seen as exemplifications of the same physical laws and are, at least in principle, calculable in their details. In atomic and nuclear physics it is likewise the aim to subsume all observable phenomena under the general laws of quantum mechanics, in particular of Schrödinger's equation. The properties of the elementary particles will one day be understood in terms of some general field equations, but there is still much work to be done before this goal is achieved. Finally it may prove possible to integrate all these general equations into a coherent whole and thus attain a complete explanation of the physical world. This is a task for the more distant future, but even if it is attained, the more limited theories of models will retain their validity as approximate but simple ways of accounting for particular phenomena.

The greater part of the day-to-day work of the scientist consists of the patient and accurate measurements of the phenomenon that interests him, together with a detailed calculation of the predictions of the various theories that have been put forward to account for it. It is one of the marks of a skillful scientist that he will, as far as possible, choose his experiments so as to make as critical a test as possible of the conflicting theories and even to decide unambiguously between them. The crucial role of the Michelson-Morley experiment in understanding electromagnetic phenomena has already been mentioned, and there are many other cases to be found in the history of science. An interesting example occurred when the nature of light was being studied. Newton had pictured it as a stream of small particles and was able to account in this way for its rectilinear propagation and even for its refraction. To account for diffraction and interference phenomena, Huygens proposed that light can also be thought of as waves. This can be formulated mathematically, and it was shown by Poisson that one of the consequences of wave theory was that if a light shines on a small smooth sphere, then there is a maximum of light intensity in the centre of the shadow on the other side of the sphere. This, it was argued, is absurd, and hence wave theory is discredited. Arago, however, was not disheartened by this and performed the experiment and found that the maximum is actually present. Thus, far from being a refutation, the argument becomes a triumphant confirmation of wave theory.

The crucial experiment that led to the foundation of nuclear physics was the study made by Rutherford in 1911 of the scattering of alpha particles by thin metallic foils. It was thought at the time that atoms are composed of protons and electrons, but the way they were arranged was obscure. Thomson had proposed that the protons were situated in a cloud of electrons rather like plums in a pudding, and this model, although crude, enabled Rutherford to show that the alpha particles would not be strongly deflected as they passed through the foils. But the results of the experiment were quite unexpected. The alpha particles were very strongly deflected, and some of them even bounced back in the direction from which they came. Since the alpha particle is about four times as massive as the proton, this is dynamically impossible on Thomson's model. It was, as Rutherford declared, as if he had fired a 15-inch shell at a piece of tissue paper, and the shell had come back at him. Such an effect could be explained only if most of the mass of the atom is concentrated in a very small volume. He thus proposed the nuclear model of the atom in which the massive protons are tightly bound together in the centre of the nucleus and the electrons form a diffuse cloud around it. By careful measurement of the scattering, he was even able to estimate the size of the nucleus; for example, for gold the nucleus is about $10^{-12}$ centimeters in diameter, while the whole atom has a diameter of about $10^{-8}$ centimeters, about 10,000 times as large.

Since that time, many other types of elementary particles have been discovered, in particular the neutrons that are also present in the nucleus with the protons postulated by Rutherford: the pion that binds the protons and neutrons together; the positron, or positive electron; the muon; the neutrino; and the whole elusive family of heavy mesons and hyperons. The complex story of these interacting investigations forms one of the most fascinating and instructive chapters in the history of physics. It is interesting to consider in more detail one or two examples that illustrate the process of discovery in a particularly striking way.

Some of these particles, like the positron, the pion, and the neutrino, were predicted theoretically before they were experimentally observed; others, like the muon, the heavy mesons, and the hyperons, were simply found, as an explorer might come upon a new species of animal or plant.

In 1930, Dirac made a detailed theory of the electron in an attempt to account for all its known characteristics. This is a difficult problem, since the electron must be described both by quantum mechanics and by special relativity. He succeeded in formulating the relativistic counterpart of the Schrödinger equation, now called the Dirac equation, and found that two of its solutions correspond to the familiar electron in its two spin states. This was exceedingly satisfactory, as it has been known for some time that these two spin states occur, but it is possible to incorporate them into the existing theory only in a rather ad hoc fashion. But he found that there were two other solutions corresponding to the two spin states of a particle that had characteristics in many respects the opposite of the electron; in particular it had a positive charge. At first it seemed an unfortunate defect of a beautiful theory that these superfluous solutions existed. Then Anderson, who was studying the cosmic radiation, noticed in his cloud chamber the tracks of particles with the same characteristics as the electron, but of positive charge. After all other possibilities had been eliminated, the existence of these particles was finally confirmed.

One of the most serious difficulties with the nuclear model of the atom was how the neutrons and protons are held together in such a small volume. The electrical forces tend to break the nucleus apart, and the gravitational forces, although attractive, are far too weak to hold it together. The electromagnetic theory had shown how it is possible to regard the electromagnetic forces as due to the exchange of photons, or particles of light; we say that the photons are the quanta of the electromagnetic field. In a similar way, Yukawa in 1935 argued that perhaps the nucleus is held together by a nuclear field with its characteristic quanta. In the same way as photons can exist apart from the particles that interact through the electromagnetic field, he suggested that the quanta of the nuclear field could also exist independently, and on this assumption he calculated the properties of these particles. They are quite different from the photon, having a mass several hundred times that of the electron and being exceedingly unstable. After many false trials these particles were finally observed in cosmic radiation. They are now called pions, and, as one might expect, they have a very strong interaction with nuclei. They have a mass about 273 times that of the electron and a mean life of about $2 \times 10^{-8}$ seconds. They decay into muons, which interact very weakly with other nuclear particles and so are frequently studied in deep mines, as it is virtually the only part of the cosmic radiation that can penetrate so far into the earth.

The methods of establishing the existence of elementary particles are perhaps illustrated in the most striking way by the discovery of the neutrino. This particle is very far from our normal human experience, and even the nuclear physicist has the greatest difficulty in forming even a vague conception of it.

The story of the neutrino began with the study of the phenomenon of beta decay, a process by which certain unstable nuclei emit an electron. The fundamental reaction postulated to account for this process is the decay of a neutron into a proton and an electron: $n \rightarrow p^+ + e^-$. This explanation is, however, unsatisfactory in several respects. The energies of the electrons vary from nucleus to nucleus, while according to the principles of conservation of energy and momentum, they should all be the same. In addition, the process does not conserve spin, since all the particles have spin one-half, and it is impossible to couple two particles of spin one-half to give a third that also has spin one-half. These conservation laws are very fundamental to the whole of elementary particle physics, and scientists are very reluctant to abandon them, though they would not be against this in principle if there were no other alternative.

To resolve this dilemma, Pauli pointed out that all conservation laws would be satisfied if an additional particle, a neutrino, were also emitted in the reaction:

$$n \rightarrow p^+ + e^- + v.$$

The properties of the neutrino could be calculated from this equation, and they turn out to be very strange indeed. It has no charge or mass, but it has a spin of one-half. Like the photon, it always travels with the velocity of light, and it also has very little interaction with matter.

This is a beautiful piece of theoretical physics, but the average experimental physicist, let alone the man in the street, is inclined to regard such explanations as rather far-fetched. But the power of science lies in the requirement that all hypotheses, however wild, should in the end always be experimentally testable.

The strange properties of the neutrino made it exceedingly difficult to test this hypothesis. One possible way is to observe the inverse reaction:

$$v + p^+ \rightarrow n + e^+$$

but this is very difficult because at the time the hypothesis was made, there was no way of producing neutrinos in large numbers, and even the interaction is so weak that the reaction would hardly ever take place.

This remained the situation until 1959, when Reines and Cowan realised that the very large numbers of neutrinos emitted from nuclear reactors made possible an experimental test of the above reaction. They devised an exceedingly complicated but crucial experiment and were able to observe, more or less directly, this inverse reaction. Their results were accepted as a convincing demonstration of the existence of the neutrino, and so this elusive particle joins the ranks of the fundamental building blocks of the physical universe. Many more experiments have been made since that time, and now no less than four different types of neutrinos have been identified and their reactions studied.

Unlike the positron and the neutrino, the heavy mesons and the hyperons were not anticipated in any way by theoreticians. They were simply observed during the course of detailed studies of the cosmic radiation. One of these particles, the kaon, presented a strange challenge when it was found that it could decay in two ways of opposite parity. Hitherto it had always been believed, on vaguely philosophical grounds, that all physical laws are invariant under the parity operations; that is, the mirror image of any experiment always gives the same result as the experiment itself. This was considered to be too obvious to doubt, and indeed it is rather difficult to devise an experiment that provides a test of the conservation of parity. One consequence of parity conservation is that a particle can decay only in ways of the same parity, and this is apparently contradicted by the kaon. The strange behaviour of the kaon prompted Lee and Yang to examine very carefully to what extent the parity conservation had been experimentally verified, and they found that the evidence was very meagre. They therefore proposed some crucial experiments, and then, when these were made, it was found to everyone's astonishment that indeed parity is not conserved in the interactions of certain types of elementary particles, including kaons, electrons, and neutrinos. It was further found that this apparent lack of symmetry in the behaviour of the elementary particles is a manifestation of a higher symmetry involving not only parity but also the change from particle to antiparticle, that is, to a particle with opposite characteristics. The anomaly in the decay of the kaon was thus explained and brought into a deeper synthesis involving not only the kaons but other elementary particles as well.

These examples all refer to the first stage of scientific discovery, concerning the establishment of the existence of the basic phenomena, and the account inevitably does scant justice to the complexity and difficulty of the original investigations. The work was accomplished by many hundreds of physicists, working throughout the world, scaling mountains and descending deep into the bowels of the earth to make their observations. Seen in retrospect, the progress may seem slow, the results simple and almost inevitable, but at the time of discovery the scientist is surrounded by a mass of fragmentary and often apparently conflicting data, and it requires years of patient work to separate the significant from the random and to weld it into a coherent whole.

The second stage is the detailed study of the properties of the particles. This requires first a knowledge of the circumstances in which they are produced, so that they can be made available at will. Ideally one would like to have well-collimated beams of the particles being studied, with facilities to adjust their energy to any required value. This can be done within certain limits for charged stable particles, like protons and deuterons, by means of the various types of nuclear accelerators. Beams of these particles are allowed to strike thin foils of various materials, and the results of the collisions are recorded in detail. By making such experiments, it is possible to obtain much detailed information about the structure of the particles and the way they act on each other. Neutral and unstable particles are much more difficult to study, so special, often exceedingly laborious, techniques have been devised to yield the requisite information.

As the measuring stage proceeds, the third stage, directed to the unifying and understanding of detailed information, becomes increasingly important. The theories of the elementary particles are still in their rudimentary stage, even though they require some of the most subtle and advanced mathematics. It is accordingly preferable to illustrate the third stage by reference to theories of the nucleus itself, since these lend themselves more readily to description in physical terms.

Several hundred types of nuclei are known, characterised by different numbers of protons and neutrons, and the properties of many have been studied in great detail. Nuclei can exist in many states of different energy and different configurations of their constituent particles. This has to be understood in terms of the interactions between neutrons and protons.

The frontal assault on this problem is simply to begin with the interactions between pairs of neutrons and protons, particles that are already quite well understood from studies of how they collide with each other away from nuclei. Then, using the Schrödinger equation, it is possible in principle to calculate the properties of the nuclei. This programme is, however, impossible for several reasons. In the first place, our understanding of the interaction between protons and neutrons is incomplete, and even if it were complete, we cannot be sure that when they are embedded in a nucleus they interact in the same way as in free space. There is a strong likelihood that the presence of other nearby neutrons and protons substantially affects the interaction. But even if this problem could be solved, we would still be faced with a mathematical problem of impenetrable complexity. It is difficult enough to solve the problem of the deuteron, consisting of just one proton and one neutron, and serious simplifications have to be made in considering the nuclei consisting of three particles. A detailed calculation of the properties of nuclei with tens or hundreds of particles is thus out of the question on mathematical grounds alone.

In such a situation the physicist makes use of models. He tries to find ways of thinking about the nucleus that can be formulated mathematically to give results that can be compared with experiment. One of the earliest models of the nucleus was to compare it with a drop of liquid. This is especially useful for heavy nuclei and has enabled us to understand to some extent how the process of fission can occur. If a drop of liquid is set into oscillation, it can in some circumstances break into two or more pieces, and the same thing can happen to the nucleus. In other respects the nucleus behaves like a gas confined to a very small volume.

When the properties of nuclei were examined carefully, it was found that in many cases there is a marked change when the number of neutrons or the number of protons has certain values, namely, 2, 8, 20, 28, 50, 82, 126, and so on. These were at first called the 'magic' numbers, since it was not known why they were important. Nuclei having 'magic' numbers of both protons and neutrons, like the alpha particle $(2n,2p)$, $O^{16}$ $(8n,8p)$, $Ca^{40}$ $(20n,20p)$, and $Pb^{208}$ $(126n,82p)$, were found to be exceptionally stable. Many calculations were made to try to understand the origin of the 'magic' numbers, and finally Mayer and Jensen postulated a certain type of nuclear force, depending on the spins of the interacting particles, that gives the numbers automatically. It was realised that the neutrons and protons can exist in certain discrete energy states, just like the electrons in the atom, and the maximum number of particles allowed in a state or shell is calculable from its quantum numbers. A magic number occurs when one shell is full of particles and there is a large separation between the highest filled shell and the next empty shell. This became known as the shell model of the nucleus. In many respects a full shell of neutrons or protons is relatively inert, so that the properties of the nucleus are largely determined by the particles outside the closed shells. Many nuclei have only one or two particles outside the shells, and it has proved possible to calculate many nuclear properties quite accurately using the shell model.

The characteristics of nuclei with many particles outside closed shells show other well-marked features that are characteristic of rotating and vibrating systems subject to quantum mechanical laws. This has led to the development of the collective models of the nucleus, so called because they postulate that nucleons move together in a collective fashion. The rotational model assumes that the neutrons and protons outside the inert core of completed shells act on the core and make it permanently deformed, like a rugby football. This can then take up energy in a characteristic way, and hence the low-lying energy states of such nuclei can be understood. In other nuclei the core is spherical when in the state of lowest energy but can be set into vibrations by external forces. Both the rotational and the vibrational energy states can be calculated quantum mechanically, and the results are frequently found to be in detailed agreement with experiments.

As our knowledge of the nucleus extends, the deviations from the predictions of the models assume increasing importance. By developing the mathematical formalism of the models, often at the expense of their imaginative intelligibility, it has become possible to account for the details of the structure of many nuclei. At the same time, the greater mathematical abstraction has allowed the interconnection between the models to be clearly seen, and indeed the shell and collective models have, at this level, been welded together in the unified model. This discussion of the methods and results of research in nuclear physics has moved far from the original question of hypothesis, theory, and certainty. Indeed the working scientist is not much concerned with these concepts as such; his attention is concentrated on the underlying reality.

The discussion of the history of the discovery of the neutrino and other particles has shown how a physical idea can progress from unsupported hypothesis to established fact. We can thus now say that these particles truly exist, although we are far from a complete understanding of their properties. This distinction between the particle and the theories that account for it is vitally important in discussions concerning whether neutrinos, or indeed any elementary particles, really exist. If by 'electron' one means the entities observed and measured by the experimentalist, then the answer must be yes. If, on the other hand, one means the subject of theories of the behaviour of electrons, then in this sense it is a mathematical construct that exists only in the minds of the theoretical physicists who use it, so that it has no independent existence. It is, however, more natural to speak simply in terms of existential electrons and the theories devised to account for their behaviour. Insofar as these theories account, however imperfectly, for the observed reality, they may be said to be partially true, but they certainly contain many aspects that are false and will be replaced by more developed theories. It is usually not possible to say exactly which characteristics of the model are true and which are false; rather, it is the whole model that is a partial and imperfect, though still useful, reflection of the underlying reality.

This contrast between the established certainty and truth of what is known and the immensity of the unknown problems that stretch out in front of him accounts for the simultaneous arrogance and humility of the scientist. He knows, like Newton, that he is but a child playing by the seashore, sometimes picking up a prettier shell or smoother pebble than ordinary, while the great ocean of truth stretches undiscovered before him. Yet these pretty shells and smooth pebbles have over the years been put together to form the vast coherent edifice of modern theoretical physics, which not only explains an immense range of sensible phenomena but underlies all our modern technology.

# CHAPTER 36

# Doubt and Certainty
# in Science

ONE OF THE MOST notable features of our times is a general weakening of belief in all those sets of values that formerly held people together and gave a sense of direction to their lives—religious beliefs, patriotic beliefs, social beliefs, moral beliefs. Groups of individuals retain strongly held beliefs, but these are contradicted by those of other groups and have no cohesive value for society as a whole. This weakening of respect for human values poses one of the most serious problems of our time.

In the midst of this flight from belief, one group stands out: A group so secure in its beliefs that it rarely thinks about them or even tries to formulate them; a group that transcends all barriers of religion, class, or nationality; a group spread throughout the world and exerting an all-pervasive influence, for good or for ill, on practically every aspect of our life and culture. This group is the scientists, the technologists, and all who share, to a greater or lesser extent, in that greater adventure of the human mind that first decisively flowered in 17th-century Europe and has led, in the intervening years, to a detailed and systematic understanding and control of our environment that is without parallel in human history.

It might, at first sight, seem an attractive solution to our problems to entrust the organisation of society to scientists. With their knowledge of the world, their careful attention to objective truth, and their concern for the future, they should be the ones to control our destiny. Yet once they are dealing with matters beyond their speciality, scientists are as prone to disagreements on social, political, moral, or ethical matters as any other group of people. Their unanimity is confined to matters that are measurable, observable, or calculable. Thus we cannot take the superficially attractive solution of letting scientists be responsible for our society; certainly with their technical expertise, they have a vital part to play, but when it comes to decisions affecting matters outside their field, they have no more to say than those trained in other disciplines.

In spite of this, we can still learn from the activity of science itself.

The remarkable contrast between the general flight from belief and the certainty of the scientists suggests that if we want to diagnose the present lack of belief, we could well start by examining the beliefs of the scientists. Why are we so sure, and how does this certainty surmount the highest barriers of culture to unite us into a single entity? What is the ultimate basis of our belief, and is it in any way similar to that of beliefs of a more traditional nature?

To do this we need to study the work of scientists to see how they try to understand the world. It is not sufficient to consult the writings of philosophers of science, partly because they reflect the main philosophical traditions and suffer from their defects, and partly because they are often so remote from the real activity of scientists that they are repudiated by the scientists themselves.

Whatever some philosophers may say, scientists are convinced that they are discovering truths about an objectively existing world and that their knowledge has cumulative character, so that we know more than the Victorians, and the Victorians knew more than the men of the Middle Ages. At any time, the scientific worldview is certainly incomplete and contains much that is only partially true or even false, but scientists are convinced that further work will gradually develop the true and eliminate the false. We believe that science has a built-in self-corrective character, that whatever fluctuation it may undergo in the difficult and uncertain processes of discovery, it is ultimately stable about the axis of truth, provided always that it remain faithful to the two essentials of logical coherence and experimental test.

This certainty comes gradually to the scientist through his long years of study and through his experiences in the laboratory. In the course of his experiments, he becomes convinced that he is in contact with an objective reality that is progressively revealed to him. He knows what it is like to struggle for months or years to understand some strange phenomenon and then suddenly to see the explanation fall into place with compelling clarity. With his new insight he can understand his observations, the apparently anomalous results fall into place naturally for quite unexpected reasons, and he can predict new phenomena and verify his predictions by further measurements. This experience has been described by Bragg when he wrote:

> When one has sought long for the clue to a secret of nature, and is rewarded by grasping part of the answer, it comes as a blinding flash of revelation: it comes as something new, more simple and at the same time more aesthetically satisfying than anything one could have created in one's own mind. This conviction is of something real, not something imagined.

No scientist who has measured the tracks of electrons or protons in nuclear emulsions or bubble chambers doubts for a moment that there are real entities that have moved along and left the tracks he sees. These are the building blocks of the natural world, and we can detect them by our instruments and measure their properties. At the close of a lecture by Rutherford, a member of the audience got up and said that he thought that alpha particles were just mental constructs postulated to correlate our sense-impressions. Rutherford almost exploded at this, and exclaimed, 'I can see the little beggars in front of me!' And so he could.

The convictions of the scientist are strengthened and deepened as he comes to understand the vast interlocking edifice of modern theoretical physics. With a relatively small number of basic concepts, he finds that he can understand and calculate to high accuracy an immense range of phenomena, mechanical and electromagnetic, atomic and nuclear. It is impossible to convey this in its fullness to one who has not mastered its discipline, but as a single example, the anomaly $a = \frac{1}{2}(g-2)$ in the $g$-factor of the electron has been determined experimentally as

$$a(experiment) = (1,159,657.7 \pm 3.5) \times 10^{-9}$$

compared with the theoretical value of

$$a(theory) = (1{,}159{,}655.4 \pm 3.3) \times 10^{-9}$$

This is like calculating the distance between London and Oxford and getting the answer correct to the nearest foot.

This is admittedly a somewhat spectacular example, and few calculations can achieve such accuracy, but it is nevertheless part of a detailed theoretical understanding of nature that encompasses the whole range of our experiences from the unimaginably tiny elementary particles to the galaxies in the vast expanses of space.

For the scientist, this experience of the power of his work is overwhelming in that it makes all other knowledge pale by comparison, and it is here that we find the basis for the faith of the scientist.

This is not to say that the scientist believes all the present content of science; on the contrary, his firm faith in science itself coexists with a cheerful scepticism concerning much of its current manifestations, particularly near the frontiers of his knowledge. Indeed he will go further and say that it is an essential part of science to consider every result and theory as to some extent provisional and subject to revision in the light of further work. It is just this flexibility and open-mindedness that gives science its strength and power of growth, so that it is always able to transcend the incomplete views of the past and to build a more comprehensive understanding in the future.

This immediately poses a problem: How can we reconcile the scientists' belief that they are continually discovering new truths about the world with their equally firm conviction that nothing they have done is sacred, that all must be considered to some extent provisional, subject to revision in light of further experience?

This leads us immediately to a central problem in the philosophy of science, an area of study that is only just appearing as an independent discipline. All too often its practitioners have been philosophers with little firsthand knowledge of scientific research or scientists with no training in philosophical method or familiarity with the history of philosophy. As a working scientist, I belong to the second of these categories, so my reflections are put forward with appropriate reservation.

In the early days of this century, the philosophy of science was dominated by the positivist school stemming from the Vienna Circle. Deploying the resources of logical analysis, they built up an account of scientific method as the construction of a series of concepts and rules that allow us to calculate observable results. Questions concerning the reality of the objects corresponding to the concepts, such as atoms and genes, were dismissed as having no meaning. This account is certainly self-consistent and covers much of the logical structure of science, but it has the disadvantage that it is emphatically rejected by the experience of the scientist himself.

More recently, another view of scientific progress has been developed by Kuhn (1970), who likens the advance of science to a series of gestalt switches, as one paradigm is replaced by another in times of revolutionary change. There is thus no meaning in enquiring whether a particular description is true or not, only whether it accounts for more or less extensive ranges of experience.

With a little oversimplification, it has been said that positivists believe in truth but not in science, while Kuhn believes in science but not in truth. Most scientists believe in both, and one problem is to give a consistent account of scientific method that allows us to do this.

One of the most notable developments of recent years has been the rise of a school of critical realists among the philosophers of science, and it is here that we find some indication of how to solve our problem.

According to this view (Harré, 1972; Wallace, 1972–74), scientific theories contain some terms that refer to hypothetical entities; these can be things like electrons or viruses, or processes like evolution or the circulation of blood. Some of these things or processes are candidates for existence: They could be real things in the world with the same ontological status as a table or a river. With the progress of scientific research, some of these candidates for reality, like atoms and bacteria, are actually shown to exist by a process of demonstration.

This account of scientific theories takes full account of the hypothetical nature of theoretical entities, particularly in the early stages. Some concepts, like force and entropy, might seem to refer to existing objects, but we later realise that they are but shorthand ways of referring to complicated ideas that are explicable only in a particular theoretical framework. Other concepts, like the postulated planet Vulcan and ether, refer to objects that could exist, but they fail the acceptance tests and are soon discarded and forgotten.

Likewise it also does justice to the conviction of the scientist that he is really finding out about how the world is constructed. He may make a hundred speculations that fall to the ground in the cold light of experiment, but just occasionally he forges a concept that passes all the tests he can devise, that gives him such a clear insight into a whole new range of experience, that enables him to understand the causes of the phenomena he observes, so that he knows that he has grasped a new aspect of reality. This account of scientific theories has a long history. From quite early times the important distinction was made between scientific explanations that provide no more than a method for computing the measurable aspects of phenomena and those that really tell us what is going on. Thus scientific explanations are of several types, ranging from those that postulate the existence of a definite entity or process, through those that suggest some correlation between concepts, such as the form of a potential, to those that postulate some very general feature of the world, such as the geometrical structure of space-time. Explanations of the first type are simply confirmed or falsified by experimental tests, though these may be difficult and take a long time. The other explanations are not susceptible to direct test and their degree of validity can be studied only through the correspondence between their myriad consequences and detailed measurements. But since it is always possible that another fundamental postulate may agree equally well, or even better, there can be no finality in this type of explanation, and it is in this domain that Kuhn's paradigm shifts are most appropriate.

This lack of finality in our abstract theoretical explanations does not affect our final certainty about the existence of the entities and processes postulated in explanations of the first type.

Examples of this process of recognition of the reality of entities first suggested as hypotheses could easily be multiplied and found in all branches of science: the neutrino, Harvey's theory of the circulation of the blood, the bacterial theory of disease, the theory of evolution, the kinetic theory of gases, and so on.

Although we are certain that neutrinos exist, and we can even identify several types of neutrinos with different properties, we are still far from understanding why such particles exist at all and why their properties are what we find them to be. We would like to unify our knowledge of elementary particles so that we could deduce all their properties from a single comprehensive theory, but we are very far from being able to do this at the present time.

This account of scientific method allows us to do full justice to the convictions of the working scientist. It recognises the provisional character of the initial hypothesis but also includes the process, known so well to the working scientist, whereby some of these hypotheses can receive such detailed confirmation that they are accepted as facts. Science is progressive in character in the sense that the number of such facts continually grows, yet at the same time the deepening of the fundamental concepts, the paradigm changes described by Kuhn, also have their proper place.

Science has evolved in the context of human history, so it is valuable to ask how and why it evolved. Science as we know it flourished decisively for the first time in 17th-century Europe, the result of a gradual growth over the previous four centuries. But why did this momentous event happen in that particular period in history? Why not in ancient Egypt, or Babylon, or India, or China? Why not among the Aztecs, the Mayas, or the Incas? This is a crucial question, for we need to understand science, and we can understand such a movement properly only if we understand its origins. If we can understand the birth of science, we can perhaps understand the reason for its vitality and its power to transcend barriers of religion, race, and culture.

The question of the origin of science is a complex historical problem that cannot be studied as the scientist would like. We cannot rerun history with different starting conditions and see what happens. We have instead to rely on our introspection and insight to evaluate the plausibility of alternative hypotheses. There are two possible approaches: First, we can see, by introspection, the essential preconditions of science, the basic attitudes to the material world that every scientist must have and without which science could neither begin nor survive. Second, we can examine in detail the great civilisations of the past and try to understand why science, in spite of several promising starts, particularly in ancient Greece, never achieved a condition of self-sustaining growth until 17th-century Europe. These two approaches are intimately linked, for only when we know the necessary preconditions of science can we see clearly why science could or could not develop in a particular civilisation.

The necessary preconditions of science are so much a part of the air we breathe that we can easily fail to notice their very special character. Science cannot exist in a vacuum; it needs a certain basic attitude to the world before it can live. These preconditions of science are neither trivial nor universal and are rarely found in human history.

The scientist must believe that the world is good, or at least neutral, that it is rational, contingent, and apprehensible. If we believed that matter is evil, we would hardly consider it worthwhile spending our lives studying it. If it is arbitrary or irrational, it would be impossible to understand it at all. If we believed its order was of a necessary kind, that it has to be the way it is, then we would hope, like some of the philosophers of old, to understand it by pure contemplation. But if its order is a contingent order, then the only way to discover that order is by the arduous road of observation and experiment. And if we believed that this order was not open to the human mind, then again there would be no point in trying to understand it.

These preconditions of science belong to the logical order, and in addition there are other preconditions that belong more to the order of action. We need a strong psychological or moral impulse before we are willing to take the trouble to understand the world. Matter does not readily yield its secrets, and without a strong external motivation, we might never get down to work, even though we recognised the theoretical possibility of attaining that understanding. Finally we must believe that our knowledge, once won, must be freely shared, for otherwise it would wither in secret and not grow from generation to generation.

All these beliefs must be firmly held before science can even begin, and, since science is a communal activity, the work of many minds, they must be held by the whole community. Thus in our search for the origins of science, we must try to find how this very special complex of ideas became embedded in the minds of the Europeans of the Middle Ages and yet did not exist in the great civilisations of the past.

This requires a very detailed study of ancient civilisations; such a study has been made by Jaki (1974). He found that without exception they were all obsessed with the idea of a cyclic universe in which after a fixed number of years all events would be repeated exactly as before, and so on forever. Such a view of the universe is intensely debilitating; if we are no more than actors in a gigantic cosmic treadmill, if all we do has already been done many times before and will be done many times again, then there is little incentive to do more than allow oneself to be carried along, listless and supine, by the stream of cosmic time.

In particular cases there are additional reasons why science did not develop, and it is important to consider this particularly in the case of ancient Greece, where science made such a brilliant start and is distinguished by many individual works of genius. The failure of Greek science was partly a consequence of the very fertility and multiplicity of ideas at that time. Isolated individuals like Archimedes and Aristotle had many of the right ideas, but they lived in a society dominated by a medley of ideas mostly destructive to science: many gods responsible for different aspects of the material world; matter as evil; history as cyclic; manual labour as fit only for slaves. So although an important start was made by a few thinkers of genius, they lacked the massive support from a homogeneous philosophy shared by the whole society.

The vicious circles of despair were decisively broken by the Judeo-Christian revelation of the one omnipotent God, Creator of heaven and earth. This immediately gave a universe with a clear beginning and end, a world of purpose, of freedom, of decision, of achievement. Such a world automatically provides the basic presuppositions, the intellectual atmosphere, into which science would be born and ultimately was born. Thus we can trace the ultimate origin of science back to the Hebrew nomads in the desert, who first learnt to worship the one true God.

In contrast to Greek polytheism, Judaism brought an uncompromising monotheism, a transcendent God who is solely responsible for all that is, the Creator of a good world. Christianity deepened the Jewish sense of purpose in history: the expectation of the Messiah, the fulfillment in Christ. Christianity brought a new attitude to work through its insistence on the necessity of transforming the material basis of life. Hence the preconditions of science, glimpsed already by the Greeks, were strengthened and unified and spread through the whole community.

The old ideas die hard, and it took many centuries of struggle before the clouds of cyclic pessimism were finally dispelled. The early Christians were not consciously preparing the way for science, but while they were preaching the word of God, they were building the outlook on the world into which it could be born. Implicit in the Gospel are new ideas about the relationships of God, man, and nature that gradually, over the centuries, brought about the conditions necessary for the birth and growth of science. St Basil, fighting the astrologers in the light of the biblical doctrine of creation, was dissipating an atmosphere inimical to science. St Augustine in his *City of God* was building a consistent framework for human existence that centuries later was to make possible the emergence of a culture with the intrinsic capacity for self-sustaining progress.

With the fall of the Roman Empire and the severance between East and West, the Muslim world inherited the riches of classical antiquity, but science failed to develop there because of the overemphasis of the Koran on the inscrutable will of Allah. Nevertheless they translated and preserved the works of the Greeks, which later formed an essential ingredient of the culture of the Middle Ages.

In the early Middle Ages the works of classical antiquity, particularly those of Aristotle, became known in the Christian West and soon came to exert a decisive influence on Christian thought. Aristotle posed many of the right questions about nature, but they could not be answered within his constricting set of ideas. The means of breaking out of this system was provided by ideas implicit in the Christian faith, and it was the fusion of Greek questioning with Christian faith that led to the birth of science.

In the beginning of the medieval period, Adelard of Bath made an important start by emphasising the rationality of the material world, saying that we must always look for a rational natural explanation before invoking the miraculous intervention of God. Later on, More, in his *Utopia*, articulated for the first time the chief components of the scientific attitude: the criticism of authorities, the use of science for social improvement, the necessity for experiment, and an optimistic faith in progress through the application of science.

The Renaissance, with its attempted revival of pagan antiquity, was a retrograde interlude, with Ficino's fondness for magic and astrology, and belief in a cyclic universe as a symptom. The Neoplatonism of Ficino's Academy reimposed the cyclic confines of Greek thought and sapped the confidence in steady progress that is an essential requirement of science.

This interlude over, the stage was set for the final emergence of science in the 17th century through the labours of Copernicus, Galileo, Kepler, and Newton, all devout Christians who were convinced that through their labours they were showing forth the glory of God. Since that time science has gone steadily forward, in spite of a lack of understanding even in the community that gave it birth.

The history of the development of science thus shows the decisive contribution made by the Christian convictions of the founders of science and of the community in which they worked. In the words of Whitehead, the Christian faith implanted

> the inexpugnable belief that every detailed occurrence can be correlated with its antecedents in a perfectly definite manner, exemplifying general principles. Without this belief the incredible labours of scientists would be without hope. It is this instinctive conviction, vividly poised before the imagination, which is the motive power of research: that there is a secret, a secret which can be unveiled.
>
> This faith in the possibility of science, generated antecedently to the development of modern scientific theory, is an unconscious derivative from medieval theology.

The theory of the origin of science suggests that it might be worthwhile exploring the connection between the presuppositions of science and Judeo-Christian beliefs.

The Christian believes that the material world is good because God made it so: 'And God saw all he had made, and indeed it was very good' (Genesis 1:31). Matter was further ennobled by the Incarnation: 'The Word was made flesh and he lived among us' (John 1:14). The world is rational and orderly because it is made by a rational God. It is contingent because it depends on the divine first; he could have made it otherwise. The world can be apprehended by the human mind, because God commanded man to subdue the earth, and he does not command the impossible: 'Be fruitful, multiply, fill the earth and conquer it. Be masters of the fish of the sea, the birds of heaven and all living animals on the earth' (Genesis 1:28).

Thus all the necessary conditions concerning the beliefs about the material world are to be found in Christianity. Christ himself reiterates the divine command to subdue the earth when by the parable of the talents he urges us to make full use of all our faculties and powers. Furthermore, as soon as it becomes clear that scientific knowledge can be applied to alleviate man's lot, it becomes a special obligation to develop it in view of the injunction to feed the hungry, to give drink to the thirsty, and to clothe the naked.

The remaining condition for the development of science, the belief that knowledge must be freely shared, is enjoined by the Book of Wisdom: 'What I learned without self-interest, I pass on without reserve; I do not intend to hide her riches. For she is an inexhaustible treasure to men, and those who acquire it win God's friendship' (Wisdom 7:13). The moral orientations of man necessary for the development of science are also to be found in Christianity.

We thus find that during the critical centuries before the birth of modern science, the collective mind of Europe was moulded by a system of beliefs that included just those very special elements that are the necessary preconditions of science. This would indicate that the connection between the Christian beliefs of the Middle Ages and the rise of science is not accidental but that there is here a real historical continuity.

This brief survey of the necessary preconditions for the birth of science and the way they were provided and implanted in men's minds may suggest that Christianity provides a view of reality that is basically sound and that if we want to restore human values, we would do well to build on the same foundations.

## References

R. Harré. *The Philosophies of Science.* Oxford: Oxford University Press, 1972.

S. L. Jaki. *Science and Creation.* Edinburgh and London: Scottish Academic Press, 1974.

T. S. Kuhn. *The Structure of Scientific Revolutions.* Chicago: University of Chicago Press, 1970.

W. A. Wallace. *Causality and Scientific Explanation.* Ann Arbor: University of Michigan Press, 1972–74.

# CHAPTER 37

# Growth and Development in Science*

THE AIM of this meeting is to reflect on the way man's understanding of a subject grows and develops from year to year and from century to century. This is a vitally important problem at the present time, when the winds of change are blowing more fiercely than ever before. These winds can blow us to ever higher knowledge and achievements, or they can blow us off course and onto the rocks.

If we are to take advantage of these winds, and not allow them to blow us where they will, we must know where we are going. We must, in particular, know how to distinguish between true and false growth, between the fruitful bud and the point of decay, between healthy development and debilitating error.

In no area is this more important than theology, for on the choices made in this generation depend the health of the Church in the future.

A time of rapid growth is a time of great opportunities. If we examine the changes that have already taken place, we may learn to see more clearly what is essential to our faith and what is not. As we grow in our understanding of the way it grows and develops through the ages, we come closer to its true nature, free from the accidents of time and place, and in this perspective we can more wisely analyse the present and lay the foundations of the future. This has an important ecumenical

---

* Peter Hodgson. 'Growth and Development in Science'. Lecture at the Farmington Institute, Oxford, November 1979.

dimension, for often the divisions between Christians concern inessentials; as we recognise this we come closer together.

In our study of growth and development in theology, we may be helped by analogies drawn from other areas of human knowledge. Already we have used the analogies of the wind of change and of a living organism. In his study of the development of Christian doctrine, Newman also made continual use of the similarity between the development of theology and that of a human person. The method of analogy is frequently used in science as we strive to understand new ranges of experience. Thus in nuclear physics we use the analogies between the nucleus and a drop of liquid and also with a miniature solar system in our attempts to understand the nucleus' structure.

The purpose of such analogies is to provide a framework of ideas that we can use to organise and classify our knowledge. The analogy, or 'model', as it is usually called, stimulates our imagination, suggests new relationships, poses new questions, and helps us to look at things in a new light and from a new point of view. It may show us what is normal and expected and what is anomalous and worthy of special study. The whole sophisticated theoretical apparatus that has been developed for one term of the analogy can be applied, with appropriate modifications, to study the new area of investigation. This method is exceedingly powerful and fruitful within science, and it is at least worth seeing to what extent it can be applied over wider areas.

Ultimately, models always break down, and we must be prepared for this. It is part of the very nature of an analogy that it shows similarities in some respects but not in others. This feature of a model is to be expected; indeed it is better not to think in terms of failure of the model but in terms of establishing its limits. To use a model successfully requires delicate discernment to deploy it to the maximum advantage while avoiding the areas where it is obviously inapplicable.

Since by its very nature a model can tell us only part of the truth, we use different aspects of the same phenomena. Where one model breaks down, another may be triumphantly successful, so by the judicious deployment of several models we can understand a much greater range of phenomena than we could with any one on its own. Ultimately, of course, we hope to attain a unified understanding, but this requires a leap forward in conceptual development. The way for this is prepared by the detailed study made possible by the various models. We thus expect our models to appear contradictory in some respects, as in the example mentioned of nuclear models. This is to be expected and does not prevent them from being extremely useful.

The idea we want to explore here is that the growth and development of science is a useful model for the growth and development of theology. We cannot at the outset be sure whether it will be any use at all. We never do when we start to use a model. We just have to go along with the idea and see if it turns out to be useful. If it does not, we just cut our losses and start again on another tack. Scientists do this all the time.

I will begin by describing science itself and the way it grows. We want to understand what is called the 'scientific method'. How does the scientist set about his task of finding out about the world? What is he doing in his laboratory when he is making experiments or in his study when he is trying to make sense of the results?

## Growth and Development in Science

It might be thought desirable to define science itself. This would be a mistake: Science cannot be neatly defined by a simple formula. It is a vast and heterogeneous adventure of the human mind, continually bursting through the neat definitions of the philosophers. We have to take science as it is now, what is accepted as scientific by its active practitioners, and analyse it as best we can. Our conclusions must therefore themselves be the product of our own times, though perhaps in some cases we can hope to attain insights of a more lasting generality.

'If you want to find out anything from the theoretical physicists about the methods they use,' wrote Einstein, 'I advise you to stick closely to one principle: don't listen to their words, fix your attention on their deeds.' This wise remark teaches us a great deal about scientists, though not much about science. It tells us that scientists are rather like cyclists, bricklayers, musicians, and most people who do things. We learn how to do it by long experience and by working with people who already know. Thereafter we carry on largely by instinct, guided by our colleagues in the scientific community. It is not part of our work as scientists to explain or to justify what we do, and we are not always very good at it when we try. As Whitehead has remarked, 'Science repudiates philosophy. In other words, it has never cared to justify its truth or to explain its meaning'.

It is perhaps interesting that there is a marked similarity between the reaction of a scientist when asked to justify his activities and that of a religious believer when asked to justify his faith or to answer specific questions or criticisms. Most of us are not really interested. No amount of clever argument would ever shake our faith, so the whole discussion is a waste of time.

If I were being really consistent I should stop at this point, but although this would be honest, it would not be very helpful or constructive. Sometimes we are bound to give an account of the faith that is within us. And of course universities are full of people with an itch to ask questions about the obvious and then to try to answer them.

It is, however, important to bear in mind that when a scientist does try to answer such questions, he is inevitably speaking outside his special competence. He is very likely to derive his answers from a half-remembered mixture of ideas about science gathered more or less unsystematically from scattered reading and occasional conversations. As a scientist, all I can really do is to describe what I do, and that would be a very long and technical story. But if you want me to answer questions about the development of science and the credibility of scientific theories, I cannot answer as a scientist. I can answer only in the framework of my wider beliefs. The answers will be different if I am a materialist or atheist or positivist or empiricist. If I were to pretend that I was answering just as a scientist, I would be deluding myself. This would mean only that my philosophy is not clearly articulated and recognised but is an unconscious half-baked muddle that has never been explicitly organised into a coherent whole.

Thus when a scientist is talking about science, except when he is being purely descriptive, he is talking from a particular standpoint of belief that lies outside science. It is essential to make this standpoint clear from the start.

I believe that science is the result of man's attempts over the centuries to find out more about the world in which we live. More explicitly, I believe that we can use our minds to find out truths about an objectively existing world. These simple statements may seem obvious enough, but there is in fact a considerable number of contrary views and much philosophical discussion concerning their truth.

Viewed in the context of human history, science is a very special achievement of man. Great civilisations rose and fell in Sumeria and Babylon, Egypt and Greece, China and India, Mexico and Peru, and in them men achieved excellence in art and architecture, philosophy and mathematics, literature and law. But in none of them did science develop into a self-sustaining enterprise. This began in the High Middle Ages and came to maturity in 17th-century Europe; it has made our civilisation unlike any other. I believe that this unique birth of science was made possible in our civilisation by Christian revelation, which taught us the fundamental beliefs about the material world that are the necessary presuppositions of science.

## The Presuppositions of Science

Science cannot even begin to exist unless the prospective scientist firmly and implicitly holds a rather special and interlocking set of beliefs about the world and about his proper attitude to it. He must believe that the world is ordered and rational and that this order and rationality are open to the human mind, for otherwise his enterprise would be foredoomed to failure. He must believe that it is good to study the world and that the knowledge he gains is precious and yet must be shared freely among all men. Finally he must believe that the order of the world is contingent, that the world could have been made otherwise, so that he cannot hope to unlock its secrets by pure contemplation but must embark on the arduous course of observation and experiment. Since science is the work of many minds, these beliefs must be held by the entire community, and this community must be sufficiently numerous and well-developed technologically to provide both the basic instruments of science and the basic necessities of life for the scientists, so that they can devote themselves wholly to their work.

These last conditions are satisfied by many of the great civilisations of the past, by Babylon and Egypt, by India and China, by Greece and Rome. Yet in none of these did science develop in recognisable form, except perhaps in a few individuals of genius, particularly in Greece. Science as we know it developed decisively in western Europe, in a Christian civilisation that taught from the beginning, as part of its message to man, just those presuppositions about the material world that we know are necessary for the growth of science.

Once science has been born, it has such inherent vitality that it can continue to develop in a wide variety of cultures, as it necessarily carries with it the view of the world that gave it birth.

In a sense these presuppositions can be said to limit science, as they make it what it is. It might nevertheless be asked what would be the effect of denying any or all of them. Could we conceive a science based on the belief that the world is chaotic and unpredictable? It would seem not to be possible to imagine what form such a science could take. (This is clearly distinct from the partial ignorance or unpredictability of statistical mechanics and quantum mechanics, which is quite a different matter.) Eddington tried to develop physics on a purely a priori basis but was not finally successful. If we believed that science was evil and should be kept secret, its days would surely be numbered. Thus the presuppositions of science seem to be essential and unchangeable.

## The Philosophy of Science

With these presuppositions, we can go on to examine science itself. This can be done in the somewhat desiccated categories of the philosophy of science, or we could concentrate our attention on what scientists actually do.

Most books on the philosophy of science are not written by scientists, and certainly they are not required reading for students of science. If scientists ever read them, they find a somewhat unreal world far from the living reality. Yet these books do contain attempts, from various points of view, to examine the logical structure of science, and so they deserve our attention. I think, however, that it is also essential to supplement this by examination of what scientists actually do when they carry out research.

The standard account of the scientific method uses the concepts of fact, hypothesis, law, model, and theory. We start our investigation by making some observations or measurements on an aspect of the world that interest us, and then we look for regularities. We make a guess or hypothesis about the underlying connections, and, if this is confirmed by further measurements, it achieves the status of a law. It is often helpful to make a model; this is essentially an analogy between something familiar and what we are trying to understand. For example, we may suppose that the nucleus of the atom is like a drop of fluid, and then we find that this helps us to understand fission. Studies of the ideas used in successful models may lead us to wider generalisations that explain a wide range of phenomena, and these are called theories. Nowadays the scientist does not have to start at the beginning; a vast body of knowledge already exists, and his task is to improve it. He may make new measurements and see if the results agree with existing theories; he may explore some of the consequences of these theories and see how well they are verified. He is always working within the framework of concepts that have been elaborated by those who have gone before him.

This brief sketch needs to be elaborated in detail, with careful definitions of the terms used and reference to a range of examples. Even then it is gravely deficient in a number of respects. It can easily give the impression that scientific research is a rather routine process and that almost anyone can turn the handle and out will come the results. Yet we know that this is not so. The essential activity of the scientist is creative; it requires insight into the structure of the world. But then we cannot describe how to be creative or to have valid insights, so our account of the scientific method breaks down at the critical point. Polanyi has pointed out that, like so many other human activities, scientific research is learnt by apprenticeship to a master. In this long process, we learn from the master in many ways that do not lend themselves to rational description; we know more than we can tell.

After these introductory remarks, we can go on to consider the actual practice of science under the headings of subject matter, point of view, techniques, and criteria of significance.

## The Subject Matter of Science

By science we seek to understand the world, and this in practice means that we try to discover regularities in the behaviour of different parts of it. The scientist is thus interested in events only to the extent that they disclose regularities, in contrast to the artist or the historian, who is interested in the particularity of each event.

Science is therefore limited to those aspects of events that display regularities that can be coordinated with similar regularities in other events. These regularities are perceived first by observation and then, on a more sophisticated level, by controlled experiment and measurement.

Any phenomenon is potentially a suitable subject for science, but it is accepted as such only when regularities become evident, preferably measurable, and fit into some theoretical framework. This is evidently so for studies of living organisms and mental phenomena, but it is true for the physical sciences as well.

The history of science provides many instances of phenomena failing to be accepted as proper subject matter for science until regularities became apparent. Meteorites were ignored by the scientific community until the evidence became irresistible. Elementary particles are accepted as physical entities only when a number of similar and evident examples have been found; one event is nearly always insufficient, as it could conceivably be explained as a series of unlikely coincidences.

Other phenomena show such erratic behaviour that they become part of science only when the detecting or measuring apparatus has been so refined that the regularities appear. It was a long struggle before electrical measurements could be made reliable, and the photoelectric effect showed its simplicity only after Millikan showed how to prepare a clean metallic surface inside an evacuated container.

Outside the physical sciences, the criteria of acceptance as a suitable subject for science are much more difficult to apply. Battles are still being fought over telepathy, extrasensory perception, and psychokinesis, recently displayed as 'spoon-bending'. It is too easy for the conventional scientist to remain aloof; probably his own discipline had an uncertain beginning.

Even in the physical sciences, it is a familiar experience in research that significant regularities are found only when the scientist knows exactly what he is looking for, when there is a theory to guide his search. The difficulties experienced where there are no such theories, as in the subjects mentioned in the last paragraph, should occasion no surprise.

## Point of View

An object or phenomenon can be approached from many different points of view, each having its own validity. A description of an object may be complete in one sense and yet entirely omit features that from a different point of view are equally important. Since only one of these points of view is the scientific one, we have to conclude that by its very nature, science can tell us about only one aspect of reality. The relative importance of this aspect is itself a question that lies beyond science. This needs to be illustrated by examples, to show in more detail the characteristics of the scientific point of view.

The scientist approaches an object or phenomenon with a desire to understand its structure, its behaviour, its physical nature. He wants to be able to define its properties in a way that can be precisely determined, and if possible, expressed numerically. He wants to understand its structure so deeply that he can calculate the measured values of its properties and express them in terms of a comprehensive theory. He would like to be able, in addition, to predict what would happen if the object were placed in a variety of different circumstances.

Thus, for example, if a scientist studies a crystal, he measures its density, its colour, its thermal and electrical conductivity, its hardness and elasticity, the angles and reflectivities of its faces, the attenuation and polarisation of light passing through it, its behaviour in electric and magnetic fields, the way it scatters light and X-rays, and so on. He will try to understand all this in terms of the atomic theory of crystal structure. Chemical analysis will tell him the constituents of the crystal, and he will postulate that these atoms are arranged in a definite lattice order. This will enable him to calculate the observed properties; comparison with the measured values enables him to check the correctness of his hypothesis. When it all fits together, he knows that he has at least some preliminary knowledge and understanding of the crystal.

He will probably find some discrepancies between theory and experiment that suggest that his knowledge is incomplete, and this will stimulate him to make more-accurate measurements and to develop his theories. He may find some entirely new way of examining the crystal, say, by neutron irradiation, and this will give him more detailed knowledge. His model will suggest new questions: Is the crystal lattice perfect, or are there some departures or dislocations from perfect order? How is the crystal formed, how does it facture, and so on?

This process is familiar to the scientist and goes on without end. His aim is to achieve as complete a description as possible.

And yet if we give our crystal to one who is not a scientist, who does not approach it from a scientific point of view, his reaction may be quite different and involve a whole new series of activities, each with its own validity in its own conceptual framework.

If the crystal is also a precious stone, a lady might think how it could be incorporated into jewellery to show its beauty to its best advantage and would wonder what clothes she ought to wear with it.

A merchant would reckon its value and to whom it might be sold. If it is a rough diamond, a cutter might begin intricate calculations to decide how it should be cut and polished to give the greatest number of finished stones.

This list is very far from exhaustive but may suffice to show that the same object may be approached from many points of view.

If this is true for inanimate objects, it is even more richly true of human artefacts and for living beings. If a scientist found a piece of paper with some marks on it, he could give a purely scientific description of it to whatever degree of detail is required. But yet he might completely miss the most important aspect of the paper, that it bears a message in an Oriental language. In practice a scientist would almost certainly recognise this—but in his capacity as a man, not as a scientist.

This is not always so, for it is sometimes disputed whether some marks on stone are primitive carvings or have a purely natural origin.

Complex experiences can be viewed in many different ways. A landscape is viewed quite differently by a painter, a botanist, and an artilleryman, and yet each is viewing the whole landscape. The configuration of waves in front of a boat is viewed differently by the alert steersman and by the relaxed passenger.

How much more does not this apply when we consider man himself? The scientific point of view alone has numerous aspects, corresponding to the range of medical and psychological specialities. Each specialist can measure and record in a most detailed way. They can extend their observations and measurements to include the dynamic aspect, how the man behaves from day to day, until ultimately they could include his whole life. But they will not consider why he was born and what happens to him after death, questions that the man himself might well consider to be more important than all the detailed scientific tests and analyses to which he has been subjected.

It is always possible for the scientist to say, when he has finished his work, that what he has done is as full a description as we can possibly have at the present time and to go on to reject any further questions as devoid of meaning. So they may be, but only to the scientist speaking as a scientist. As soon as he thinks as a man in the fullness of his human nature, he knows that the other questions insistently force themselves upon his attention.

## Techniques

An essential part of science is the techniques used to obtain the results embodied in the scientific view of the world. These range from the careful observations of the biologist to the sophisticated measurements of the physicist. While precise measurement is not an essential component of science, it is characteristic of its highest development, and the very high precision achieved in many branches of the physical sciences is an essential condition for their breadth of understanding and detailed predictive power.

It is necessary that all the techniques of the scientist be generally accessible and repeatable, so that anyone anywhere with the necessary equipment and skill can repeat the experiment and verify the results. This is true over a whole range of the sciences and is not affected by apparent exceptions provided by rare natural events, like eclipses or supernovae.

No result is accepted as part of science unless it has been checked independently by two or more scientists; until this is done it remains provisional. No scientist can claim some special technique that is his alone. This is not, of course, to say that all observers are equally competent; naturally some are more skillful than others, and they obtain results whose reliability and accuracy depend on their skill.

This requirement of universality is one reason it is so difficult to make a scientific study of phenomena like psychokinesis and extrasensory perception, which appear to be associated only with certain individuals in particular circumstances. For the same reason a unique personal experience, however impressive to the recipient, cannot be considered science.

## Criteria of Significance

It is quite possible to make observations and measurements in a fully scientific way on things or processes that are valid objects of scientific study and yet obtain results that have no scientific significance at all. Thus if I count the number of dead matches on the road as I walk along, my result may be perfectly accurate, but it is not a scientific result, unless perhaps it has some minuscule sociological significance.

This is in essence the fundamental error of the Baconian method: that one has simply to make a large number of observations and measurements and then try to unify them into a science. In fact we have to be extremely selective in our observations and measurements, and on several different levels.

On the lowest level, our scientific work must be directed to proper objects of study from the scientific point of view, as outlined in previous sections. Then from all the infinite number of measurements that could be made, the scientist must try to select the most significant. This is the most difficult part of scientific research, not only because the significance of a piece of research is apparent only when it is complete, if then. Yet somehow a scientist must judge whether a piece of work is worth doing before he begins, and this requires experience, flair, luck: It is an art not easily acquired.

To guide him in his selection, the scientist has available the state of knowledge at the time, as embodied in books and papers, conferences, and discussions with other scientists. He must know the current experimental situation and state of development of the theories and hence can judge what experimental work still needs to be done and what aspects of the theories should be tested. If he is thoroughly immersed in this, he knows the sensible things to do, what research would be accepted for publication in a respectable journal. If his work does not satisfy this condition, it is not serious scientific work. In a rapidly expanding branch of science, this means that work that was perfectly respectable at one time is inadmissible a few years later. Practising scientists would dismiss it with pity and would regard the author as not knowing the score.

This criterion serves to define what is science at a particular time but still leaves open a vast range of possibilities, and it is here that the judgement of the scientist comes into play. So far he has needed only a knowledge of the literature and an understanding of the state of development of his subject; now he has to exercise much more subtle skills, and it is mainly at this level that the real abilities of the scientist show themselves, distinguishing the really able from the merely competent. The aim is to identify the lines of research that will lead to a new discovery or to the development of a theory that will throw new light on the subject. Once the choice is made, the actual carrying out of the research is a much more straightforward matter, depending on technical ability, patience, and other assorted skills.

These are the criteria of significance that apply in the planning stage of research. Other criteria come into play when the results begin to appear. It is rare that a piece of research has a well-defined termination. The first results may tell the scientist whether this particular work is likely to bear much fruit; if they are unpromising, he may decide to cut his losses and start something else. If they are promising, he will continually alter his plans to improve their accuracy and significance. He will compare them with existing theories as soon as he can and thus find out how the measurements should be refined to give results of even greater significance.

The criteria at this stage are also on several levels, not always easy to discern. A simple comparison of theory and experiment seldom gives perfect agreement, even allowing for the statistical errors. If there is a glaring discrepancy, this is a highly significant result that may force the modification or even abandonment of the theory. More often the disagreements are small, and it is then a matter of judgement whether to ignore them as being due to some unexpected interference or to follow them up in more detail, making more measurements of higher precision. Here again considerable judgement is needed. It is quite impossible to follow up every small discrepancy, and yet many times in the history of science very small effects have been the first indications of important discoveries or even of whole new branches of science.

So far the criteria of scientific significance have been considered only within the existing framework or paradigm. Most science is of this character, but occasionally the reigning paradigm is found increasingly inadequate and is finally replaced by a better one, as happens at times of revolutionary change. The work leading to such changes is of the highest importance, and yet just because it conflicts with the contemporary paradigms, it may at first be rejected as unscientific. Many examples of this have occurred in the history of science.

The new paradigms are not easily accepted by those immersed in the old, but the criteria of significance are the same as those previously applied, namely, the requirement that they make sense of our experiences and enable us to correlate and predict them in a quantitative way.

It is interesting to observe that these criteria of significance, of many types and on many levels, are never codified or taught to young scientists. They are not provided with a handy rulebook to tell them what is scientific and what is not or how they should decide what research to embark on next.

The reason for this surprising omission is perhaps the general unphilosophical character of scientists, or perhaps the sound intuition that such codification is more likely to be stultifying than inspiring.

## Beyond Science

So far the limits of science have been defined by considering the inherent nature of scientific activity, which by itself imposes limits on the types of questions that can be posed and answered by the scientific method.

An alternative approach is to consider what areas of activity are by their very nature beyond the limits of scientific enquiry. To the extent that these are recognised as real, this also tells us about the limits of science. What follows is by no means an exhaustive list; it simply provides a few illustrations that can easily be multiplied.

The first activity that comes to mind is philosophical discourse about science itself. This paper, for example, is certainly not a scientific paper, so if it has any meaning, it must be accorded a different status. The history of science, and indeed all history, is distinct from science because it is concerned with events in their unique particularity, whereas science is interested in events only insofar as they exemplify general principles.

The whole area of moral judgements likewise lies outside science. It is possible to observe and describe human actions, but it is not possible from within science to say whether these actions should or should not have been done; this can come only from outside science. This is the familiar distinction between 'is' and 'ought' statements. There have been attempts to derive a morality from the practice of science itself by saying that one always ought to behave in the way most conducive to the development of science. Besides leading to some unacceptable conclusions, such as legitimising medical experiments on unwilling people, this line of reasoning is valid only if we first accept the supreme value of science, a judgement that itself lies outside of science. Thus we conclude that the whole area of moral judgements lies outside science.

This is not to say that morality is no concern of science. On the contrary, it is essential to its healthy life. The Christian revelation that did so much to prepare the way for the birth and growth of science provides also the morality that makes possible its development. The virtues of truthfulness, patience, modesty, perseverance, openness, courage, and optimism are all needed by the working scientist if he is to do his work well. They do not of course by themselves guarantee success, and many of them are also extolled by the other great religions of mankind.

Finally, there are the pressing questions of the ultimate destiny of man, no less insistent in spite of the difficulty of answering them. How is it that on this small planet there have arisen beings able to probe and partially understand their world, driven by a restless curiosity to explore the inner recesses of the atom and the vastness of galactic space? What is the ultimate purpose for which we should live our lives?

These are insistent questions, and though our scientific work can help us in numberless ways, we must find their answers beyond the limits of science.

## Growth and Development of Science

The day-to-day growth of science is full of error and confusion, and it is only gradually, with immense difficulty, that the truth emerges. The scientist has to try out hundreds of ideas before he is lucky enough to find one that is useful. In order to make any progress at all, he must not be afraid of making mistakes. To get his research going, he must make some initial hypothesis, and it will almost certainly turn out in the end to be wrong. But, in the very process of testing and refuting it, he will have attained a new vantage point that will perhaps suggest a more refined hypothesis, and so on. In this process, the scientist always strives for precision and clarity. If an idea is sharp enough to be useful, it must be sharp enough to fail and be proved wrong, or at least inadequate. It is useless to put forward a hypothesis that is so vague and general that it cannot be subjected to a decisive test. As Bacon has remarked, truth emerges more readily from error than from confusion.

The actual conduct of research is a delicate interplay between theory and experiment, between the ideas and concepts and their testing by experience. It is far more difficult and complicated than one might suppose from books on scientific method. There are endless possibilities for misinterpretation. Incorrect theories sometimes fit the data very well, and experiments often give misleading results. The born scientist seems to know by instinct what is wrong and where the truth lies and is able to discard ideas and results that conflict with what he knows to be true. It is far too simple to say that we discard a theory that disagrees with experiment. Very often scientists have held on to a theory in the teeth of contrary results and have in the end been vindicated.

There are two extreme models of the growth of science: One sees it as a process of continual accretion, like the building of a house; the other sees it as a series of revolutions that every now and then completely alter the way we think about the world. Both models are inadequate, the former because it does not take into account all the blind alleys in the advance of science or of the far-reaching conceptual changes that occasionally take place, and the latter because it denies the underlying continuity and real sense in which each generation can say it knows more about the world than its predecessors.

Most of the time, science advances fairly steadily within a particular set of ideas about the world. At rare intervals, this set of ideas has to be profoundly modified when experiments show that the old view is no longer tenable. An example of such a change is the replacement of Newtonian dynamics by the theory of relativity in the early years of the 20th century. Here we have both radical change and underlying continuity. The relativistic concepts of space and time are profoundly different from those of Newton, and yet, in the limit of small velocities, Einstein's equations always give the same results as those of Newton. Thus the actual equations of Newton retain their validity for small velocities, and yet we have refined our ideas of space and time so that we can also deal correctly with high velocities as well.

The really important ideas in science are the work of individual men and women of genius, but their work would be impossible without the less spectacular work of thousands of others. This has been well emphasised by Rutherford, himself an innovator of genius:

> It is not in the nature of things for any one man to make a sudden violent discovery; science goes step by step, and every man depends

on the work of his predecessors. When you hear of a sudden unexpected discovery—a bolt from the blue as it were—you can always be sure that it has grown up by the influence of one man on another, and it is this mutual influence which makes the enormous possibility of scientific advance. Scientists are not dependent on the ideas of a single man, but on the combined wisdom of thousands of men, all thinking the same problem, and each doing his little bit to add to the great structure of knowledge which is gradually being erected.

There is at the present time intense discussion among philosophers of science concerning the development of science, and particularly by Kuhn, Feyerabend, Lakatos, and Holton. It might well be thought that it is necessary to master these and similar writings before venturing an opinion concerning the growth of science. However, we notice that the scientific community continues with its work oblivious, for the most part, to the writings of the philosophers. We don't take any notice of what they say. We can therefore find at least part of our answer by examining the workings of the scientific community, which corporately is responsible for the growth and development of science.

The scientific community is a believing community, a body of men and women devoted to studying the world in its various aspects. In some respects this community is very informal; in other respects it is highly organised. There is no written credo of beliefs, yet they are no less strong for not being explicit: They become clearly evident when challenged. Many examples could be given of how the scientific community has reacted very sharply when attempts have been made to influence scientific conclusions on the basis of considerations external to science, whether political, ideological, or practical.

The scientific community is quite well defined. There is a long novitiate, culminating in a university degree. The initiation into research takes many years, and the completion of the first stage is usually marked by a doctorate. After that, one remains in the community as long as one continues to carry on research or to teach.

The community itself decides how science is to grow and develop. Each scientist may decide on his own research project, but the results of his work are accepted as part of science, and even then in a probationary sense, only when they are published in a reputable journal. The people who decide what is to be accepted as genuine science are thus the referees of the papers, who are asked by the journal's editor to give their considered opinion on the originality, technical accuracy, and scientific value of the papers sent to them. The author must show that he is fully aware of the previous results in the same field and must put his work in its proper context. This does tend to put a premium on rather unexciting work along well-trodden lines. A really new idea has a much rougher passage and has to be markedly successful before it is accepted. Scientists know very well that most new ideas turn out to be wrong, but in that very small fraction proved correct is found the seeds of future progress. The history of science is full of examples of the initial rejection of ideas that later proved to be of the highest importance. Most scientists are rather strongly influenced by authority when new ideas are being considered. If put forward by someone who is relatively unknown, the ideas are not likely to be taken seriously. If, however, they are put forward by a respected scientist, with years of sound work to his credit, they have a much better chance of gaining an initial hearing.

The other important area of decision for the growth of science is appointments to temporary or permanent posts in universities and research institutes. These decisions are usually taken by a committee of experienced scientists, who examine the record of research submitted by the candidate and try to estimate his originality, ability, and technical skill. Thus essentially all decisions concerning the growth and development of science are taken by more-experienced scientists acting as members of the community.

How can we distinguish between true and false science, between growth and decay, between brilliant insight and perverse aberration? These are vital questions that go to the very heart of science. Our criteria are interlocking and mutually reinforcing, but we may perhaps distinguish several distinct aspects. They do not provide an instant touchstone to separate the true from the spurious; often this is by no means obvious at first, and it takes time for the status of a particular development to become clear.

In the day-to-day progress of research, the criteria of a true development are, first, the obvious ones of internal consistency and accord with experiment. More-subtle criteria are the requirements of simplicity and beauty, always the hallmarks of advances of great power and generality.

In a more systematic way, the criteria of true development may be summarised under four headings.

### Science Is One

Truth is one and so science is one. Measurements of the same quantity give the same results. At the first International Conference on the Peaceful Uses of Atomic Energy, the American and Russian delegations revealed their highly secret data on the properties of uranium: They were the same within statistical uncertainties. There may be two theories of the same phenomena, but sooner or later one of them will be shown to be wrong, or they will be found to be equivalent, or they both will be transcended by a higher theory.

### Science Is Fruitful

A true development is one with the potential for abundant growth. It stimulates a range of new experiments and theoretical speculations. Relativity and quantum mechanics are outstanding examples of fruitful developments. By contrast, a false development simply dies.

### Science Is Universal

Perhaps more than any other human activity, science transcends all boundaries of race, language, nationality, and culture. Scientists from all around the world understand each other immediately if they are working in the same field, and information is exchanged freely between them. This has been called an 'invisible college'.

### Science Is Continuous

The development of science is a continuous historical process from the time of its birth until the present day. Each scientist has learnt from his predecessors and would have been able to do very little without their help. Even the most eminent scientists are dependent in this way. As Newton remarked, we all stand on the shoulders of giants.

These four characteristics of the growth and development of science may be compared with the four marks of the church: one, holy, Catholic, and apostolic. The further study of this analogy and its applications is a task for theologians.

# CHAPTER 38

# Humility at the Heart of Physics

THE ACHIEVEMENTS of modern science and technology are so impressive and influential that they may cause us to think that all problems can be solved by the scientific method and that problems that cannot be so resolved are meaningless pseudo-problems.

Such naïve confidence in the universal power of science is less noticeable nowadays because it is increasingly evident that society is confronted by a series of intractable problems that cannot be solved by scientific methods alone and also that there are real human problems forever beyond the reach of scientific enquiry. It is therefore useful to try to clarify the limits of science, so that we can see what problems we can reasonably expect it to tackle, and which must be faced, if at all, in other ways.

Scientists give the impression that they are arrogant. They are certain that what they say is true and brush aside any objections. To some extent this is justified when they talk about their own speciality but not when they talk about other aspects of science and even more when they talk about politics and other matters of general concern.

When they are researching in their chosen field, scientists take great care to make their experiments as accurate as possible, and they check and double check their own and other scientists' results. They can make mistakes, but in the end the result is reliable knowledge. They have established a feature of the way the world is, whether we like it or not.

The results scientists obtain may not be what they expected and may even go against their previous beliefs. Max Planck, the founder of quantum theory, came from a very conservative family of scholars. He realised that the frequency distribution of the radiation emitted from a hot body is a very fundamental feature of nature. It had been measured very accurately, and he wanted to understand it.

The existing theories gave a good account of the measurements for high and low frequencies but not for the region between. Planck succeeded in finding a mathematical formula that fitted the spectrum very accurately. He then tried to derive it theoretically by assuming that the radiation comes out in small bundles, and he planned to obtain the final result by letting the size of the small bundles go to zero. To his astonishment, he found that this gave the wrong result, whereas assuming that the bundles are finite gave the correct one.

This result went against all his instincts as a physicist, and he tried for years to get round it but without success. He was thus forced to admit that radiation is emitted in bundles that are now called quanta. In this he acted as a true scientist, humbly accepting the facts. Scientists do not impose their ideas on nature; they accept what they find and publish their conclusions. They are understandably angry if someone who knows nothing about the subject contradicts them, and this can give the impression of arrogance.

It is quite a different matter if a scientist speaks in a dogmatic way on matters outside his speciality. He is, like anyone else, entitled to his opinions but has no monopoly on the truth. Unfortunately there are many scientists who use their scientific authority to lend weight to their views on political or moral questions. Even within their speciality, it is prudent to speak with caution and always to be willing to give reasons for their conclusions. This is far more necessary in other matters.

Other examples are provided by scientists who deny the need for a Creator on the basis of some very speculative theories and by others who say that evolution just happened by chance, without ever defining 'chance'.

Quite often a declaration on some matter of public concern is issued with the signature of a thousand scientists or a hundred Nobel

Prize winners. It is then important to ask whether each of these scientists really has a specialist's knowledge of the subject of the declaration. If not, they are acting arrogantly.

Scientists do their best to find out about the laws of nature, and they cannot alter what they find. It is no use asking them to alter the law of gravity. If you ignore the law of gravity and jump off a cliff, you get hurt. That is the way the world is, whether we like it or not. Similarly it is no use asking the Church to alter the moral laws. In both cases we just have to try to live our lives in a way that respects both the laws of nature and the moral laws.

Scientists sometimes attribute more finality to the present theories than they really deserve. Toward the end of the 19th century, many scientists thought that physics was almost complete, and that all that remained was to make some more measurements to achieve a higher accuracy. The young Planck, contemplating his choice of career, hesitated between philology and physics and was advised to choose philology because there was nothing more to be done in physics. Eminent scientists are prone to adopt the same attitude even now, saying that the formulation of a final theory of everything is just around the corner. A little knowledge of history ought to show them how unwise are such statements.

Another example is provided by quantum mechanics, which Niels Bohr believed to be the final theory, the end of the road in physics. By this he meant that no improved theory is possible, so that the wave function contains all that can ever be known about a physical system. This not only gives rise to the quantum paradoxes, but it implies that it is forever impossible to find any hidden variables that specify the deterministic system that underlies the indeterminism of quantum mechanics. In this way Bohr set up a barrier against further progress. Recently, however, there has been renewed interest in deterministic theories of physics such as the pilot wave theory and stochastic electrodynamics. The latter has the merit of providing a physical model of the deterministic substratum and a possible way to resolve the quantum paradoxes.

A dramatic illustration of the debilitating effect of Bohr's attitude is provided by the story of Rutherford's attempts to find the structure of the nucleus, following his successful discovery of the structure of the atom. Bohr told him that it was a fruitless task, since the interior of the nucleus is a structureless soup; all we know is that sometimes particles are emitted from the nucleus; any questions about nuclear structure are simply meaningless. Discouraged by all this, Rutherford gave up the search. We now know that the instruments available to Rutherford were not sufficiently precise to obtain evidence of nuclear structure, but his insight was confirmed when a decade or so later the shell structure of the nucleus was discovered. Once again humility, the refusal to be discouraged by preconceived ideas about what is and what is not possible, had shown its power in scientific research.

The concept of humility had indeed been elevated to a principle many years earlier by the physicist and mathematician Sir Edmund Whittaker when he proposed what he called his postulates of impotence as the foundation of all physics.

Thus physics and chemistry are based on the impossibility of creating or destroying mass and energy, now combined as mass-energy. Thermodynamics, and with it much of physical chemistry, can be deduced from the postulate: '[I]t is impossible to derive mechanical effect from any portion of matter by cooling it below the temperature of the coldest of the surrounding objects'. Fundamental to mechanics is the impossibility of perpetual motion, and to relativity the impossibility of detecting absolute velocity. The theories of electricity and magnetism can be derived from the impossibility of establishing an electric field in any region enclosed by a conductor and charging the outside of the conductor. Together with the postulate of impotence underlying relativity, it is possible to derive the inverse square law of motion between stationary electric charges and, then, the existence of magnetic forces, and, finally, Maxwell's equations of the electromagnetic field. Whittaker observes that a postulate of impotence is not the direct result of an experiment, nor is it a statement of mathematics. It asserts the conviction that 'all attempts to do a certain thing are bound to fail'. Eventually, Whittaker believed, we may look forward to a time when all of physics can be deduced logically from a few postulates of impotence. This might be thought to be the final demonstration of the value of humility in physics, but it is pride rather than humility to anticipate such a final achievement. We can never exclude the possibility of yet another experiment that could give a result inconsistent with such a final theory. Humility must always remain at the heart of physics.

In all areas of life, if we want to learn anything, we must be attentive, receptive, humble, and willing to set aside our preconceived ideas, our prejudices, our hopes, and our fears. 'Unless you become as little children you shall not enter the Kingdom of God'.

# CHAPTER 39

# Superstitions

WE ALL TEND to believe that we live in a scientific age and that superstitions belong to the past. We laugh at the medievals with their beliefs in charms and omens and at the rainmaking ceremonies of primitive peoples.

And yet if we look around us, superstition is as rife as ever. Go into any popular bookshop and you will find entire bays devoted to the occult. The shelves devoted to serious science are few compared to those with books on science fiction. Open a popular magazine and you will find pages devoted to astrology and horoscopes. These tell you, according to the sign of the zodiac under which you were born, whether this will be a good month to embark on a new business venture or whether you can expect some misfortune to befall you. Such things flourish because we all yearn to know the future and want to find ways to influence it in our favour.

Why should anyone believe these superstitions? It is relatively easy to test their truth value. If, for example, a specific prediction is made for a certain category of people, one can see whether that prediction is eventually fulfilled or not. If it is fulfilled in a sufficient number of cases, then it is reasonable to take such predictions seriously in the future. This is a rational and scientific way to investigate such subjects. It would be useful to make such tests and publish the results, although it would be optimistic to expect that they would have the desired effect.

Scientists, as well as all sensible people, are dismayed at the vast proliferation of various superstitions and the number of people who take them seriously. In 1975, 186 scientists, including 18 Nobel Prize winners, published a condemnation of astrology. They warned the public against accepting the predictions and advice given by astrologers and asserted that their beliefs had no scientific foundation. They lamented that in these enlightened times, belief in astrology still pervades our society. In spite of their efforts, astrology flourishes, and it is difficult to see how it could ever be eliminated.

In making this statement, the scientists were almost certainly correct. Astrology is an evil that should be eliminated. And yet it should be pointed out that the scientists themselves were behaving in a very unscientific way, one that could even be called superstitious. First of all, why collect 186 signatures? Would not one valid argument be sufficient? Furthermore, there is no mention in the statement of any experimental investigation that proves the falsity of astrology. It is indeed highly unlikely that any of those scientists ever made such an investigation. And yet it is an essential part of science that if one is faced by a problem, one makes careful experiments before coming to a conclusion.

The scientists, in making their statement, were not reporting the results of experiments; they were asserting conclusions based on their beliefs about the world. This is rather similar to the actions of the astrologers, who also make statements based on their beliefs about the world. The fact that the beliefs of the scientists are probably true and those of the astrologers are probably false is not the point. The point is that if one is going to make any statements, either about what will happen in the future or on the credibility of astrology, they must be based on objective scientific studies. Neither the astrologers nor the scientists provided them.

# CHAPTER 40

# Motives

A MAN once encountered three men working and asked them what they were doing. The first replied that he was breaking stones; the second responded that he was earning money to feed his family; the third proudly said, 'I am building a cathedral'.

We often do things for a mixture of motives, and sometimes the most important, the driving, motive is not the one we advertise. It may even be hidden from ourselves.

What motives should inspire a scientist? It often happens that a boy or girl is captivated by the beauty, elegance, objectivity, and power of mathematics and by the way it can be used to solve physical problems. In mathematics a problem has a definite, exact, and certain answer. Physics provides a way of solving problems about the behaviour of matter in a similarly exact way. It is all so different from other subjects, where discussions go on and on without ever coming to clear and definite conclusions.

This may lead to the decision to become a scientist, and then one has the opportunity to discover things about the world that have never been known before. It is an unforgettable experience to make even a small contribution to knowledge, and it more than compensates for all the difficulties, trials, and frustrations inevitably encountered on the way to a discovery. This is a cause worthy of the devotion of a lifetime.

Scientific research is an exciting quest. Richard Feynman once remarked that the work is not done for the sake of an application. It is done for the excitement of what is found out. You cannot understand science and its relation to anything else unless you understand and appreciate the great adventure of our time. You do not live in your time unless you understand that this is a tremendous adventure and a wild and exciting thing.[1]

As time goes by, other motivations come to the fore. It is necessary to obtain an income to provide the necessities of life. Fortunately, there are various institutions that support scientists in return for services such as teaching and that allow time for research.

Scientific knowledge is good in itself but can also be applied in numerous ways. Over the last few centuries, it has transformed our lives. This gives society an additional incentive to support scientists. The geese that lay the golden eggs must be fed.

At this point an insidious danger arises. Scientific research is expensive, so is it not very reasonable to support only those projects that will give results that benefit society? Thus when scientists apply for support, they are more and more often asked to specify the benefits that are likely to accrue.

In this way the motivation of the scientists is twisted. No longer do they seek only to understand the natural world; instead, they want to use it for the benefit of mankind.

This is an insidious danger because it sounds so reasonable. Many religions and philosophies have taught that the natural world should be studied only to find ways to solve practical problems. It is found in the Koran and also in Marxism and is one of the principal reasons for the abysmal level of science in Islamic countries and the relatively poor state of Soviet science. The insistence on practical motivation is a sure road to mediocrity and leads in the end to the death of science.

It is easy to give examples of this. If Roentgen had been told to improve methods of medical diagnosis, he would never have studied electrical discharges in gases, which led to the discovery of X-rays. If Faraday had been told to improve transport, he would never have made the first electric motor.

---

[1] Richard P. Feynman, *The Meaning of It All* (London: Allen Lane, Penguin Books, 1998), 9.

The Russian physicist Landau once said, 'One must never work for ulterior motives—for fame, or with the aim of making a great discovery—nothing will come out of it anyway'. The scientist Szent-Gyorgyi said that he would throw out of his laboratory anyone who said he wanted to do research in order to help mankind. No motive other than finding out about the world is acceptable. 'Seek ye first the kingdom of God'.

# Subject Index

# Name Index